Publishing Your Psychology Research

A guide to writing for journals in psychology and related fields

Dennis M McInerney

SAGE Publications
London • Thousand Oaks • New Delhi

Published in 2001
Allen & Unwin
83 Alexander St
Crows Nest NSW 2065
Australia

SAGE Publications Ltd
6 Bonhill Street
London EC2A 4PU

SAGE Publications Inc
2455 Teller Road
Thousand Oaks, California 91320

SAGE Publications India Pvt Ltd
32, M-Block Market
Greater Kailash – I
New Delhi 110 048

British Library Cataloguing in Publication data

A catalogue record for this book is available from the British Library

ISBN 0 7619 7336 2
ISBN 0 7619 7337 0 (pbk)

Library of Congress catalog record available

Typeset in 10/11.5 pt Arrus by DOCUPRO, Canberra
Printed by South Wind Production Services, Singapore

CONTENTS

Acknowledgments   *v*
Introduction   *vii*

1 Quality in psychological research: What journal
   editors are looking for   1
2 Quality problems and issues in major types of research   12
3 Selecting a journal outlet and submitting your article   28
4 Writing your literature review for an effective article   57
5 Writing your method for an effective article   74
6 Writing results and discussions for an effective article   89
7 The review process 1   99
8 The review process 2—responding to reviewers'
   comments   111
9 From thesis to journal article   129

Appendix   *Code of ethics*   *137*
Index   *142*

ACKNOWLEDGMENTS

I wish to acknowledge all the wonderful researchers who have published clear and powerful studies that have acted as exemplars for my own work. I also want to acknowledge all the editors and reviewers who have responded to my work and given me insights into what makes a piece publishable. In particular, I want to thank Professor Herbert Marsh for sharing with me many of his insights into research publishing that have helped shape my own attitudes and skills. Finally, I want to thank Elizabeth Weiss for her warm encouragement in this project, Rebecca Kaiser for her excellent contribution to the design and publication of the book, and to the three reviewers of the manuscript for their excellent suggestions which improved the text.

INTRODUCTION

At the outset I want to say this is *not* a research methodology book. There are many excellent methodology tests available and I do not want to proliferate these. However, what is lacking is a text that guides the competent early researcher through the maze of getting published.

While it has always been important for academics to be published if they wished to contribute to, and disseminate, knowledge in their field of expertise, the imperative to be published is stronger today than ever before. There are a number of reasons for this, not the least being the way in which funding to universities internationally is allocated partly in terms of research productivity and output. Furthermore, promotion and progression as an academic, in most university settings, requires an academic to be a productive researcher. Productivity is most often measured through the vigour and depth of one's research program that is reflected in the quality (and quantity) of research publications, as well as through the research grants awarded to the researcher. Hence the 'squeeze' is on all academics to be productive research writers.

But few academics are taught how to write their own research to maximise its potential for publication. Indeed, statistics reveal that in many research fields the average per annum publication rate per individual is very low.

Research publishing is tough. As an academic psychologist I learnt through trial and error what to do and what not to do in order to be published. This book is written for the individual who wishes to have the process 'de-mystified' and 'de-terrorised'. I take the reader step-by-step through the publication process. First, I illustrate how to read research in psychology intelligently so that the exemplars can act as models for personal research writing. Second, I illustrate how to design research so that it has potential for publication. Third, I take the reader carefully through the process of writing research so that it may be published in the appropriate and 'best' journals. There is not much use doing research unless it is published. Even commissioned 'commercial and in confidence' research should be publishable in the best journals, albeit there might be an embargo on publication. If the research is not good enough to be published then it should not be done. If it is good enough, then this book should help it see printers' ink (or cyber space representation).

The book is written in an accessible style and should appeal to a wide audience from raw beginners through to seasoned veterans who have the responsibility for training the researchers of the future and who will pass the book on to graduate students and novice researchers. It should also be of interest to professionals in general, administrators and consultants. There is limited technical information (such as on methodologies and statistical descriptions) and these are used for illustrative purposes—eg, to illustrate where individuals can make flawed presentations which will preclude their article from being reviewed and accepted for publication. In each chapter there are excerpts from published research and editorial/reviewer comments as examples. Many of these are chosen from my own work. The reason for this is not a 'big head' as many of the examples are negative ones, but rather, it is less problematic to obtain copyright permission to reproduce one's own work.

I hope the reader enjoys the book and finds it a valuable introduction to the world of research publication. I welcome any comments.

1

QUALITY IN PSYCHOLOGICAL RESEARCH: WHAT JOURNAL EDITORS ARE LOOKING FOR

- The heuristic value of research
- Being knowledgeable about research
- The stages of the research process
- Contributing to research—student, novice and experienced researchers
- Ethical standards of research

THE HEURISTIC VALUE OF RESEARCH

If you are reading this book you are probably a budding researcher or a mentor of budding researchers. You might also be a proficient researcher, just curious about the nature and purpose of this book. In any event, it is important for all researchers to examine the purpose and importance of research in their areas and their particular role in it. Research is usually associated with acquiring new knowledge through empirical means. It is also associated with change, development, and more often than not, progress in a particular area. In most areas of human endeavour there is formal and informal research dedicated to issues of interest, significance and importance. Let's look at a few examples. There is extensive and continuing research in an incredibly wide range of medical areas. Some of these are very high profile areas, such as AIDS and cancer research, while many others are less high profile, but nevertheless of great significance such as research on palliative care. There is also extensive and continuing research in the

1

sciences, for example the research effort of groups such as CSIRO and NASA, and many other scientific organisations. Again, much of this research is very high profile, such as that on genetically modified food and cloning. There is extensive research in areas dealing with social and personal areas such as family life, health, education and religion. And finally, there is research in business, economics, religion, politics, sports and defence. In other words, research occurs in most, if not all, areas of human activity.

We need to ask the question therefore, why do humans conduct research? Of course, one impelling reason that research is conducted is human curiosity: human beings are intensely curious. Even our forebears with sloping foreheads were researchers when they put their fingers into fire to explore the quality of flames, and discovered (when their yelping had subsided) various uses for heat that have become refined over the millennia. Humans also found that the study of the world around them allowed them increasing control of the natural elements. This control led to benefits including improved standards of living and increased longevity. In other words, there is a strong link between research and human progress.

This increase in knowledge generated through investigation and discovery led directly to the establishment of universities and schools to conserve, pass on, and further develop human knowledge, much of it acquired through research. And this is probably where you are sitting now—in a university, pondering the value of research and your role in it.

BEING KNOWLEDGEABLE ABOUT RESEARCH

In order to be an effective researcher one has to be knowledgeable about research. Indeed, being knowledgeable about research is a value in itself, whether or not one is an active researcher. We are all consumers of research information and it is a good idea to know how to distinguish good research from indifferent research and poor research. Among the basic issues we need to attend to when reading research are the quality and value of the issues being investigated, the quality and appropriateness of the methodologies chosen for the investigation, and the quality of the analyses and the reporting of the results of the investigation. As you will see later, these are also key elements in the writing of research. Let's look briefly at each of these elements.

Quality of the issues being investigated

There is an element of subjectivity in making an evaluation of the quality and value of particular research. I have attended many university research committee meetings, vetting research funding applications, where very heated arguments have ensued on whether a particular project is sufficiently worthwhile to spend hard money on. Some of the 'muddying' features in these arguments relate to whether the research has the potential to make a contribution to knowledge; whether there is any applied value in the research; whether the research has already been done; whether the researcher demonstrates competence and a background in the research area; and whether the research has a place in the grander scheme of things (whatever this might mean). It is not only at these funding meetings that such evaluations occur. Whenever a research author submits reports for presentation or publication in refereed fora, reviewers are usually asked to comment on the quality and value of the research. I have just completed a series of reviews on proposals for an international refereed research conference that included the following checklist:

Importance of			
problem/question	insignificant	1 2 3 4 5	significant
Theoretical framework	none	1 2 3 4 5	well-grounded
Contribution to field	minor	1 2 3 4 5	major

When you are reading research you will be making judgements about each of these issues as well (or at least you should be), and I will be giving guidance throughout the book on how you might make informed judgements. Certainly, when you are preparing your own research projects, and finally writing the results for publication, you would want to be assessed as straight fives. Again, I hope to provide you with insights that will enable you to adapt your writing skills in ways likely to enhance the probability of publication.

The quality and appropriateness of the methodologies chosen for the investigation

It is axiomatic that good research should be founded on appropriate methodologies. A good research question will go nowhere without this foundation. In considering whether a methodology is appropriate (there might be several appropriate alternatives) you must consider the nature of the research questions asked. The research strategies used by the researcher must be clearly linked to these specific research questions and issues. Research questions and issues dictate the nature of the data to be acquired. The nature of the data to be acquired influences the method chosen to gain these data, and the type of analyses to be conducted. Central, therefore, to the research design is the research issue.

There are a number of methodologies for conducting research. Among these are experimental designs which attempt to truly control the experimental variables and seek for causal relationships; quasi-experimental designs which do not have the same level of control but also seek to examine cause and effect; and correlational designs which are concerned with prediction and the association between variables. There is also a wide range of qualitative designs such as case studies, observational studies and ethnographies that are becoming increasingly popular in psychological research. Each of these approaches has its strengths and weaknesses. The task of the researcher is to maximise the strength of an approach while minimising (or controlling for) any weaknesses that might be present. Most importantly, the researcher must match the research design to the research question and the type of data available. Your task as a reader of research will be to assess how well this has been done in a particular study. If it is not done well, then the research will be compromised.

Data are, of course, the raw material of the research. The researcher must decide what types of data are most relevant to answer their research question. Data may be scores on a test, reaction times to a stimulus, rankings on a performance, preferences and attitudes and observations. Given this, the researcher needs to decide how the data are to be quantified, analysed and interpreted. The decisions made will influence the quality of the research and its validity. A research question being answered with poor data will founder.

As indicated before, when research is being reviewed for publication a checklist might include such criteria as:

Does this manuscript add to
our knowledge in an
important way?   (No) 1 2 3 4 5 (Yes)
Are the theoretical aspects of
this work clearly developed
and relevant to the empirical
findings reported?   (No) 1 2 3 4 5 (Yes)

Are the empirical aspects of the work appropriate given its theoretical context?	(No) 1 2 3 4 5 (Yes)	
Have the empirical aspects of this work been properly carried out?	(No) 1 2 3 4 5 (Yes)	
Is the statistical treatment of the data appropriate?	(No) 1 2 3 4 5 (Yes)	
Are the data appropriately interpreted?	(No) 1 2 3 4 5 (Yes)	
Are alternative interpretations of the data identified, discussed and/or appropriately controlled?	(No) 1 2 3 4 5 (Yes)	
Is relevant literature cited and appropriately discussed?	(No) 1 2 3 4 5 (Yes)	

THE STAGES OF THE RESEARCH PROCESS

At the risk of oversimplifying the process of empirical research and its reporting, I will briefly describe some identifiable stages in the process. These will be developed in greater detail in later chapters as I explore the ways in which these elements of research are to be effectively written for publication.

Identifying a problem

As I have suggested above, a research issue or problem forms the core of any research program. You should be able to clearly identify the research issue in any research report you are reading, and be able to clearly enunciate the research problem in any project in which you are engaged. This research issue or question should be substantial and capable of sustaining your interest throughout the project. It goes without saying that it is very important for you to be able to clearly articulate the purpose for your research in any article you write for publication. We will examine means of doing this in later chapters.

Reviewing the literature

It is important to ascertain whether the research question has already been identified and answered by other researchers. It is futile to spend time and resources on a problem that has already been solved! Presuming that the research issue is still 'live', it is very important to review literature related to the problem. This review may suggest potential avenues for investigation, partial solutions, and appropriate methodologies, tools and analyses. In other words, the background literature will provide the researcher with a good foundation upon which to construct the study. Again, you should be able to ascertain from the literature review in a particular study where this study fits in the advance of knowledge in the particular area. We will explore elements of effective literature reviews for publication in Chapter 4.

Constructing the research design

The research design will be comprised of the research questions, an identification of the appropriate data to be gathered and the method for this, and the analytical tools and approaches for analysing the data. Again, each of these must be consistent with the research aims. In addition to these are associated concerns such as whether you have access to the type and size of sample you need, how long the study will take, how expensive data entry and analysis will be, what special equipment is needed, and so on. A time and resource line that clearly focuses on these issues is always helpful to guide your research. Each of these elements must be clearly presented in any paper written for publication. We deal with these issues in Chapters 5 and 6.

Completing the study

Once all is in place, the researcher will complete the study. This will include collecting the data, carrying out appropriate analyses, interpreting these analyses and the writing of the final report. I am particularly concerned in this book with the writing of the final report for publication. However, as I have indicated above, unless each of the elements of the research design is appropriately carried out, there will be little possibility of the research being published in reputable refereed journals.

CONTRIBUTING TO RESEARCH—STUDENT, NOVICE AND EXPERIENCED RESEARCHERS

Every researcher begins as a student and hopefully progresses from novice to experienced. At each level, a contribution can be made to research development. If you are a student, you will seek to acquire the skills of research from appropriate mentors and exemplars (such as good research publications). In learning you will also challenge those guiding you to practise and mentor effective research skills. In a sense, the mantle of responsibility for conducting good research is being passed to you and therefore those responsible for your development should have the future in mind. As a novice researcher, you will actively contribute to various research projects, perhaps through an honours or doctoral program, or as a newly appointed researcher. As a novice, you will bring a fresh approach to the research enterprise and perhaps have exciting insights into new problems and methodologies. Finally, as an experienced researcher you will have mastered each of the elements of good research design, and will be making a contribution to the expansion of knowledge.

ETHICAL STANDARDS OF RESEARCH

An overarching concern in conducting psychological research should be the ethics of what we are doing. Early in your career as a psychological researcher, you need to become familiar with the ethical standards of research appropriate to our profession. All universities have established ethics committees to preview research from this perspective, and research may only be conducted under the auspices of a university if it has ethics approval. Furthermore, psychological societies and funding agencies have also published guidelines for conducting ethical research. I do not intend to go into detail here on the ethical standards appropriate to your research as you can readily access this information through your organisation or funding body. What I do want to draw your attention to is that ethical standards also apply to publishing the results of your research. Authors submitting articles to journals published under the auspices of the American Psychological Society routinely receive the following letter. It clearly enunciates important ethical standards that you should consider before turning your research into a research article.

Dear Colleague:

This letter is being sent routinely for information purposes to everyone who submits an article to an APA journal. Please feel free to distribute it to your colleagues and students. The scientific literature is our institutional memory. It is important that this literature accurately reflect what happened, who did it, and to what extent one observation is independent of another. APA is seriously concerned about the integrity of our literature and has included an expanded section on publication in the 1992 revision of the APA Ethical Guidelines, which took effect December 1, 1992. (See Ethical Principles of Psychologists and Code of Conduct, 6.21–6.26). We can prevent problems before they occur in two major areas addressed in these guidelines. One deals with plagiarism; the other with duplicate or fragmented publication.

Plagiarism. Authors should cite the sources of their ideas and methods as well as put quotation marks around phrases taken from another source. The change or reordering of a few words in a sentence does not relieve authors of the obligation to quote and recognize appropriately the source of their material. As recent cases inform us, authors need to be scrupulous in their note taking (especially in the electronic form) and careful about using those notes in their own manuscripts.

Duplicate/fragmented publication. Duplicate publication involves publishing the same data more than once. Fragmented (or piecemeal) publication involves dividing the report of a research project into multiple articles. Duplicate or fragmented publications are misleading if they appear to represent independent observations. They can distort the scientific literature, especially in reviews or meta-analyses.

On occasion it may be appropriate to publish several reports referring to the same database. The author should inform the editor at the time of submission about all previously published or submitted reports so the editor can judge if the article represents a new contribution. Readers also should be informed; the text of an article should include references to other reports using the same data and methods or the same sample or portions of it.

Sometimes authors want to publish essentially the same material in different journals in order to reach different audiences. There is little need for this practice now that we have computerized retrieval systems to search the literature, and such duplicate publication can rarely be justified. If you think it may be, the article must include reference to the original report—both to inform editors, reviewers, and readers and as a necessary fulfillment of the author's obligations to the previous copyright holder.

In general, the author should inform the editor about the existence of other reports from the same research project at the time of submission. If you are in doubt, please consult with the editor.

Sincerely,
APA Chief Editorial Advisor

You should also consider the following standards for reporting and publishing scientific information which should guide your research and writing. (See also the code of ethics for psychological research produced by the Australian Psychological Society, reproduced in Appendix I.)

The following ethical standards are extracted from the 'Ethical Principles of Psychologists and Code of Conduct.' which appeared in the December 1992 issue of the *American Psychologist* (Vol. 47, No. 12, pp. 1597–1611). Standards 6.21–6.26 deal with the reporting and publishing of scientific information.

6.21   Reporting of Results
(a) Psychologists do not fabricate data or falsify results in their publications.
(b) If psychologists discover significant errors in their published data, they take reasonable steps to correct such errors in a correction, retraction, erratum, or other appropriate publication means.

6.22   Plagiarism
Psychologists do not present substantial portions or elements of another's work or data as their own, even if the other work or data source is cited occasionally.

6.23   Publication Credit
(a) Psychologists take responsibility and credit, including

authorship credit, only for work they have actually performed or to which they have contributed.

(b) Principal authorship and other publication credits accurately reflect the relative scientific or professional contributions of the individuals involved regardless of their relative status. Mere possession of an institutional position such as a Department Chair does not justify authorship credit. Minor contributions to the research or to the writing for publications are appropriately acknowledged, such as in footnotes or in an introductory statement.

(c) A student is usually listed as principal author on any multiple-authored article that is substantially based on the student's dissertation or thesis.

6.24   Duplicate Publication of Data

Psychologists do not publish, as original data, data that have been previously published. This does not preclude republishing data when they are accompanied by proper acknowledgment.

6.25   Sharing Data

After research results are published. Psychologists do not withhold the data on which their conclusions are based from other competent professionals who seek to verify the substantive claims through reanalysis and who intend to use such data only for that purpose, provided that the confidentiality of the participants can be protected and unless legal rights concerning proprietary data preclude their release.

6.26   Professional Reviewers

Psychologists who review material submitted for publication, grant, or other research proposal review respect the confidentiality of and the proprietary rights in such information of those who submitted it.

Multiple authorship

In my treatment of writing research I will, in general, refer to you as the first or sole writer. It is increasingly common that articles are authored by a number of researchers. However, the guidelines I give in the following chapters are relevant whether you are a sole or joint author of research articles. In the next chapter I discuss the types of research you might conduct and implications for publication.

2

QUALITY PROBLEMS AND ISSUES IN MAJOR TYPES OF RESEARCH

- Basic and applied research
- Research methods
- Validation studies
- Qualitative research
- Integrative reviews and meta-analyses
- Research design and potential for publication

Research in psychology takes many different forms. The form of the research dictates, in many ways, the nature of the research article that is written to report on the research. In this chapter I will give a brief description of some quality issues related to the major types of research from the point of view of potential for publication. I must emphasise that this chapter does not explore these methodologies in any depth. There are numerous excellent methodology books available to you, and you are probably very familiar with these. Nevertheless, my thumbnail sketches of the major components of the approaches will refresh your memory, while highlighting key aspects that need to be well developed in research articles.

BASIC AND APPLIED RESEARCH

Before we consider specific methodologies, it is necessary to consider basic and applied research. It is common to make a distinction between what is called basic (sometimes called 'pure') and applied research. Indeed, in many grant applications the researcher is asked to indicate the type of research and the proportion that might be described as basic, and the proportion that might be described as applied. Some grants may only be awarded to one or other form of research. It is also common for journals to specialise in publishing one or other type of research.

What is basic research? What is applied research? At its most simple level, basic research deals with the generation of new knowledge or the extension of existing knowledge. It might be an experiment examining the impact of x on y, or a study of the attitudes of individuals to a particular issue. The focus is clearly on what new information is provided by the research without regard to immediate practical application of the knowledge. The research may even appear somewhat unrelated to 'real world' issues and the solving of specific problems.

Applied research, as its name implies, is concerned with the application of knowledge to solve specific practical problems. For example, once it is discovered that x has a particular effect on y, other researchers may attempt to use this information to solve a relevant problem. Indeed, the progress of much medical and scientific practice proceeds in this way. There are many examples of basic research having a dramatic impact on our everyday lives through the clever application of new information to old problems. For example, the discovery of recency and latency effects regarding recognition and recall resulted in communication theory advocating that the delivery of information is more or less effective when given in chunks using the seven, plus or minus two, rule.

As I indicated above, some journals specialise in one or other form of research. The journal *Basic and Applied Social Psychology* deals with both, and as you will see from the following editorial, sees its role as synthesising the strengths of both.

From the Editor . . .
Basic and Applied Social Psychology

As I begin my term as Editor for *Basic and Applied Social Psychology*, I would like to make clear some of the goals and ambitions that I have for the journal. Foremost, of course, I hope to carry on the fine tradition established by past editors who have shaped the journal into a respected publication for basic and applied research in the social sciences. Since its inception 17 years ago, the journal's mission has been to provide a forum for the best work on the boundary between basic and applied social psychology. That mission grows increasingly more timely. We live in an era of enormous social and technological change. Rather than neatly solving society's ills, technological advances have made more apparent the vital role that social scientists will play in tackling the major problems that face us. Social science research that is carefully conceived and can inform us about potential and real avenues of application will be particularly relevant. *BASP* will continue to be a home for this research. Perhaps the biggest challenge will be maintaining the fragile but healthy balance between the twin emphases that make *BASP* a unique outlet in which social scientists can publish their work. There is always a danger that basic research will lose touch with the 'so what?' that should guide it and that applied work will lose sight of the 'why?' that guarantees effective implementation. I hope that the powerful interplay between these two emphases will be apparent in all of the work that we publish.

You should be able to ascertain from the abstract of articles their research emphasis. You need to be clear in your own exposition of your research whether the emphasis is basic, applied, or a combination. Usually this is first communicated in the abstract of your article. I have included below two brief abstracts representing basic and applied research. See if you can distinguish between the two!

Abstract

A connectionist model of an atonal discrimination task is reported which illustrates the fundamental principles of artificial neural networks and embodies the assumptions of pattern recognition theory. Musical sequences are defined as patterns consisting of local and global features and it is proposed that recognition of music is achieved by way of processes which extract and differentially weight such features. Musical training serves to refine the feature extraction and weighting processes. As hypothesised, musically trained and untrained listeners were able to discriminate between atonal sequences on the basis of rhythmic and intervallic features although there was no effect of musical training on accuracy and response time measures. Neural network and human data were compared and testable predictions generated by the mechanistic model are provided. The potential contribution of connectionist models to developmental and environmental aspects of music perception and cognition is discussed.

From Stevens, C. & Latimer, C. (1997). Music recognition: an illustrative application of a connectionist model. *Psychology of Music*, 25, 161–85. Reprinted with permission.

Abstract

The specific aim of this research was to determine whether the goals held by students from diverse cultural backgrounds differ, and the relationship of these goals to school motivation and achievement. Five groups of high school students were selected, Australian Aboriginal ($n=496$), Australian Anglo ($n=1$ 173), Australian immigrant ($n=487$), Native American Navajo ($n=529$), and Canadian Betsiamite Indian ($n=198$). Participants completed a self report instrument (the Inventory of School Motivation) based on goal theory. Confirmatory factor analyses were conducted to establish the adequacy of the instrument for use across the selected groups. Group differences were analyzed through the application of ANOVA. Finally, multiple regression analyses were conducted to examine the relationship between the goals held by the participants and school achievement criteria. Our findings suggest that the model is applicable across the four groups; that motivational profiles of the diverse groups are more similar than different; that a narrow range of goals and sense of self variables are important in explaining school achievement on educational criteria, and these are similar across the groups; and that key variables used to distinguish Western and indigenous groups do not appear to be salient in the school contexts studied here.

From McInerney, D. M., Roche, L., McInerney, V. & Marsh, H. W. (1997). Cultural perspectives on school motivation: the relevance and application of goal theory. *American Educational Research Journal* 34, 207–36. Copyright (1997) by the American Educational Research Association; reproduced with permission from the publisher.

RESEARCH METHODS

Below the level of basic and applied research are the research methods that researchers choose to conduct their research. There are three methods that I wish to introduce briefly here. You should obtain a good methodology book to examine each of these in more detail. I have included a list of recommended texts at the end of this chapter. Three approaches that are commonly used in psychology are experimental research, quasi-experimental research and correlational research. Each approach has its specific requirements and is suited to particular research questions and settings. Furthermore, when you come to write up the reports on your study the description must include essential elements that will describe the research as experimental, quasi-experimental or correlational. If these are not described correctly the article will be rejected. I want to emphasise here that I am not discussing your ability to conduct effective research using an appropriate methodology, but rather the importance of clearly presenting features of the method you have used in the written form. It is quite common that well-conducted research fails to be effectively translated into well-written research papers.

Experimental research

In experimental research the researcher manipulates one or more independent variables (those chosen as important by the researcher) in order to observe their effects on one or more dependent variables (outcomes seen to be important by the researcher). All other variables that might have a confounding effect on outcomes are controlled. So, for example, the researcher might be interested in the effects of reaction time of individuals to blinking red and green lights. Variables that might have an impact such as sex, age, disabilities and so on, are either built into the experiment as independent variables, or controlled if they are viewed as confounding. Control might be achieved either through randomising or counterbalancing the variables, if the sample is large enough, or matching and holding them constant. Extraneous elements that might also have an unwanted effect (such as time of day, room distractions etc.) are also controlled so that the direct effects of red and green lights on reaction time are validly measured.

There are a number of experimental designs used by researchers. These deal with issues such as the number and arrangement of independent variables, the number of levels of each independent variable and the way the levels are selected, the way subjects are selected and assigned to conditions, how confounding variables are controlled for, and finally a description of the statistical analyses used to evaluate the results of the experimental manipulation, including details on statistical significance and effect size. It is very important for the researcher to clearly describe the research design and statistical analyses used in any publication coming from the research. This is important to facilitate the journal editor's assessment of the validity of the research, the generalisability of the findings, and to facilitate replication by other researchers. In psychology there are numerous examples of well-conducted experimental research. The following abstract illustrates experimental research. Naturally, in the method section of the article the experimental features are described in greater detail. We explore this further in Chapter 5.

Abstract

In the work reported in the literature the reduction or decrement in the magnitude of the Muller-Lyer illusion with continued inspection has been typically investigated with the use of the composite illusion form. Three experiments are reported in which the illusion decrement was separately examined in the underestimated (wings-in) and the overestimated (wings-out) forms of the Muller-Lyer illusion, with particular attention paid to the transfer of illusion decrement between the two forms. Decrement occurred in both forms of the Muller-Lyer illusion, although there was considerable variability in decrement effects, and nonuniform rates of decrement across the inspection period. In none of the experiments did transfer of illusion decrement between the two forms occur. It is argued that the attentional/differentiation hypothesis of illusion decrement provides a plausible account of the present findings as well as of those found with the composite Muller-Lyer figure.

From Predebon, J., Stevens, K., & Petocz, A. (1993). Illusion decrement and transfer of illusion decrement in Muller-Lyer figures. *Perception*, 22, 391–401. Copyright (1993) from Pion Limited, London; reproduced with permission from the publisher.

Quasi-experimental research

At times in psychological research it is not possible to control all variables that might be extraneous to, but have an effect upon, the observed outcomes. Furthermore, the interactive effects of a whole range of variables (such as socio-economic status, educational level of parents, culture, prior educational experiences) might not easily be either controlled or manipulated in an experimental design. This is particularly the case when the researcher conducts an experiment with human participants in intact groups. In other words, the researcher has less control over matching and randomisation. It is common for classroom experiments to be quasi-experimental as the researcher has little control over who is in each class. For example, if a researcher wants to examine the effects of an 'old' and 'new' way of teaching by comparing the outcomes in two classes, there is a more limited possibility for experimental control. Nevertheless, well-planned quasi-experimental research can have many of the hallmarks of experimental research, by incorporating as many principles of scientific control as possible given the circumstances. Well-planned quasi-experimental research, for example, can allow for pre–post comparisons, some randomisation to groups, some matching, and various statistical controls over the data to eliminate variance due to extraneous features of the design and sample. In fact, in some cases, the distinction between true experimental and quasi-experimental research is tenuous. The following abstract illustrates quasi-experimental research. As with experimental research, it is important for you to clearly and fully describe the details of the experimental conditions, including any special materials used, the selection of the samples, and the techniques employed by you

Abstract

Two aptitude–treatment interaction studies examined the comparative effects of metacognitive strategy training in self-questioning within a cooperative group learning context and a traditional direct instruction approach, on the acquisition of computing competencies, learning anxiety, and positive cognitions. When prior competence in using computers is controlled, students' initial aptitudes interact significantly with teaching method. Cooperative groups scored significantly better on achievement tests, self-concept, and sense of control–mastery than did the direct instruction groups. Paradoxically, for the initially high-anxious learners, some aspects of computing anxiety remained high in the cooperative group relative to the direct instruction group, suggesting that anxiety may facilitate learning.

From McInerney, V., McInerney, D. M. & Marsh, H. W. (1997). Effects of metacognitive strategy training within a cooperative group learning context on computer achievement and anxiety: an aptitude–treatment interaction study. *Journal of Educational Psychology*, 89, 686–95. Copyright (1997) American Psychological Association; reproduced with permission from the publisher.

to control for confounding due to extraneous factors outside your control.

Correlational research

Both experimental and quasi-experimental research are concerned with demonstrating causal relationships. That is, the experimenter sets out to demonstrate that if variable *x* is manipulated in a particular way it will have a causal effect on what happens to variable *y*. Not all psychological research is amenable to such an approach, nor is all research able to clearly isolate causality. The focus of much psychological research is to demonstrate relationships between variables, such wise that as variable *x* varies, variable *y* varies in some predictable way. This type of research is called correlational research. For example, in my research I examine the relationship between academic motivation and school achievement. As academic motivation is enhanced, school achievement should also be enhanced. In other words, academic motivation and school achievement should covary. However, this relationship does not demonstrate causality for a number of reasons. First, another, unexamined variable might be 'causing' the changes in both; second, the cause could go in either direction, that is, when a student is highly motivated he or she achieves more, or as a student achieves more he or she becomes more motivated; and third, the covariation could be reciprocal. Hence, from simple correlational designs it is not possible to demonstrate causality, although many novice researchers imply this from their findings. This does not mean that this style of research is of no value. The covariation of variables is heuristic for examining the dynamics of many behavioural outcomes from a psychological perspective. There are also a number of more complex correlational designs that do enable the researcher to examine causality, particularly with multi-wave data. Structural equation modelling, for example, is a sophisticated statistical and methodological tool for structuring data so that effects of x on y can be examined. A discussion of these approaches is beyond the scope of this text. The following abstract represents correlational research. Again, the description of your design must be detailed in the method section of your article.

Abstract

The aim of this research was to determine whether the goals held by students from diverse cultural backgrounds differ and to determine the relationship of these goals to school motivation and achievement. Participants completed a self-report instrument (the Inventory of School Motivation) based on goal theory. Confirmatory factor analyses were conducted to establish the adequacy of the instrument for use across the selected groups. Group differences were analyzed through the application of ANOVA. Finally, multiple regression analyses were conducted to examine the relationship between the goals held by the participants and school achievement criteria.

From McInerney, D. M., Roche, L. A., McInerney, V. & Marsh, H. W. (1997). Cultural perspectives on school motivation: the relevance and application of goal theory. *American Educational Research Journal*, 34, 207–36. Copyright (1997) by the American Educational Research Association; reproduced with permission from the publisher.

What is most important for you to consider as a writer of research is that each of these methods must be clearly described in research reports, and that the generalisations of findings are in keeping with what the method really allows the writer to say. As I discuss later, journal editors are very sensitive to inappropriate designs and the presentation of misleading findings. While most research writers will put the 'best gloss' on their design and analyses it is essential for you to clearly address the issue of what variables could or could not be controlled and the compromises involved in various levels of control. It is also important for you to discuss the limitations in your statistical analyses and to provide appropriate caveats on your research findings. This ultimately has to do with the validity of the findings. When you ignore these issues you jeopardise your article's potential for publication.

VALIDATION STUDIES

At times a major feature of a study might be the validation of a new instrument or methodology. At other times researchers may subject existing instruments to validation checks to see how effectively they stand up to the claims made of them by their authors. In general, most journals do not publish validation studies if these are the major or exclusive focus of an article. However, there are a number of journals that do specialise in publishing these such as *Applied Psychological Measurement*, *Educational and Psychological Measurement*, *Journal of Educational Measurement*, *Psychometrika* and *Structural Equation Modeling*. These journals provide a valuable service as they provide detail on the validity and reliability of new and existing instruments so that future researchers can choose to use these in their research programs. The following abstract represents a validation study in psychology.

Abstract

This article discusses the process through which a powerful multidimensional measure of affect and cognition in relation to adult learning of computing skills, the Computer Anxiety and Learning Measure (CALM), was derived from its early theoretical stages to validation of its scores using structural equation modeling. The discussion emphasizes the importance of ensuring a strong substantive basis from which to develop reliable items for a measure as well as the usefulness of gathering qualitative data in both the factor and item design stages. The final instrument comprises 11 first-order factors and 1 negative item factor. These can be more parsimoniously represented as 5 factors, 2 of which are second order, and a measurement–method effect. Although tests of factorial invariance across different faculties provide considerable support for the stability and generalizability of the model, future research would need to examine whether the CALM model is invariant across different adult populations in similar computer learning/training environments.

From McInerney, V., Marsh, H. W. & McInerney, D. M. (1999). The designing of the computer anxiety and learning measure (CALM): validation of scores on a multidimensional measure of anxiety and cognitions relating to adult learning of computing skills using structural equation modeling. *Educational and Psychological Measurement, 59,* 451–70. Copyright (1999) by Sage Publications, Inc.; reprinted by permission of Sage Publications, Inc.

QUALITATIVE RESEARCH

The research designs we have considered so far are quantitative designs in which statistical analyses play a large role. One difficulty with such approaches is that they can be somewhat removed from the real world of human experience. Increasingly in psychological research, researchers are using alternative methods to address questions which take a more naturalistic bent. Sometimes these alternatives are used in the early stages of research to examine a problem in its 'real' or 'normal' context in order to generate plausible hypotheses, or appropriate tools (such as survey questions) for later experimental or correlational research. They are also used to understand or check on findings, particularly ones that are counter-intuitive, that is, they can be used to test hypotheses and provide information to supplement, validate, explain, illuminate or reinterpret quantitative data. And at other times these approaches are considered to be the essential means by which a problem can be effectively addressed because they allow the examination of a problem holistically, taking account of real life in all its complexity and depth. In this latter case, for example, the researcher might be specifically interested in the perceptions of the participants 'from the inside' which could not be effectively addressed experimentally. In general, these methods, referred to as qualitative, use relatively little standardised instrumentation and do not depend on extensive statistical analyses.

Qualitative research has a long and illustrious history in psychology. Many of the key theoretical perspectives guiding psychology have been derived from qualitative analyses. I only need to mention Freud, Piaget, Vygotsky, Jung, Kohlberg and Kuhn for you to realise the rich informative contribution made by these theoreticians to our understanding and awareness, and importantly, our view of human personality and development.

Qualitative research may be biographical, phenomenological, ethnographic, and case study, and based on grounded theory. Data may be obtained through archival records, oral histories, interviews, autobiographies, studies of individuals and their lived experiences, surveys, observations, fieldwork studies and so on. As with quantitative data, the aim of the researcher is to reduce the data (and with qualitative research this can be quite extensive) into meaningful patterns. And for each approach, therefore, there will be related data analysis techniques, such as coding and content analyses of documents and scripts. Increasingly there are available computer software packages that facilitate the analysis and interpretation of qualitative data. As with good quantitative research the researcher needs to control extraneous variables and ensure that spurious results are not generated by the analyses. There are many excellent qualitative research texts around and you should consult a number of these if you are interested in conducting qualitative research. As with quantitative research, it is essential for you to fully describe your methods including the conceptual frameworks you used to organise your variables and their relationships, the research questions posed to define the objects of your enquiry and set boundaries on your study through case definition, how you planned for within-case and multiple-case sampling, how you created your instrumentation, and how you alleviated biases in your study. Again, details on these aspects of your research are essential for the journal editor to evaluate the objectivity, reliability, validity and transferability of your research and its findings. The following research by an educational psychologist illustrates the use of qualitative research to expand our understanding of the reading process.

Abstract

Joshua, a second grader at the preprimer level, resists answering the author's questions about his conceptions of reading until she agrees to spend equal time drawing and looking through Waldo books with him. Surprisingly, it is while 'doing Waldos,' rather than during classroom observations or in answering her carefully planned interview questions, that Joshua shows the author his developing sense of narrative, his earliest attempts at phonetic decoding, and the importance of minimal-text books like Waldo books as a nonthreatening gateway into literate experience for him and other struggling readers. The author comes to see such shared agenda setting as not just the most ethical way to interview people but also the most effective, because it allows for the serendipity of discovering answers to questions the author had not even thought to ask.

From Knapp, N. F. (1999). Interviewing Joshua: on the importance of leaving room for serendipity. *Qualitative Inquiry*, 3, 326–42. Copyright (1997) by Sage Publications, Inc. Reprinted by permission of Sage Publications, Inc.

A major difficulty with reporting qualitative research is that reports tend to be overly long. Many authors strenuously resist suggestions by editors and others to reduce the length of their article. The upshot of this is that relatively fewer qualitative articles are published. If you are doing qualitative research you must become quite pragmatic about what is really essential reading for your readership and discipline yourself to write in a succinct and fluent fashion. There are some excellent examples of published qualitative research in psychological journals and you should use these as models.

INTEGRATIVE REVIEWS AND META-ANALYSES

While you might not typically think that a literature review is a form of research, reviews that involve a secondary analysis and synthesis of data across related studies are, in fact, very valuable forms of research. All researchers depend on both integrative reviews and meta-analyses to describe what findings are already available on particular topics and how other researchers conducted their studies. We discuss the importance of this in Chapter 4 dealing with writing literature reviews. An integrative review is one that primarily synthesises and interprets findings on a topic across a range of relevant research articles. It will identify themes, and may discuss the strengths and weaknesses of particular articles and the field of research as a whole. A meta-analysis goes further. It takes the primary statistical findings from a large number of research projects related to a specific topic, such as the effect of self-esteem enhancement programs on academic achievement, and derives a measure which reflects whether, on average, results are significant or not, and positive or negative. Both forms of literature review are very useful for researchers developing a research program as you will see from the two extracts below. Many researchers believe that research effort ought to be expended on consolidating the abundance of research findings already available. In this way, they argue, the consolidation of knowledge may contribute new and important insights from psychology. The first extract represents an integrative review, and the second a meta-analysis.

Abstract

The purpose of this article is to examine the contribution made by the self-efficacy component of Bandura's (1986) social cognitive theory to the study of self-regulation and motivation in academic settings. The difference between self-efficacy beliefs and other expectancy constructs is first explained, followed by a brief overview of problems in self-efficacy research. Findings on the relationship between self-efficacy, motivation constructs, and academic performances are then summarized. These findings demonstrate that particularized measures of self-efficacy that correspond to the criterial tasks with which they are compared surpass global measures in the explanation and prediction of related outcomes. The conceptual difference between the definition and use of expectancy beliefs in social cognitive theory and in expectancy value and self-concept theory is then clarified. Last, strategies to guide future research are offered.

Abstract

The effects of within-class grouping on student achievement and other outcomes were quantitatively integrated using two sets of study findings. The first set included 145 effect sizes and explored the effects of grouping versus no grouping on several outcomes. Overall, the average achievement effect size was +0.17, favoring small-group learning. The second set included 20 effect sizes which directly compared the achievement effects of homogeneous versus heterogeneous ability grouping. Overall, the results favored homogeneous grouping; the average effect size was +0.12. The variability in both sets of study findings was heterogeneous, and the effects were explored further. To be maximally effective, within-class grouping practices require the adaptation of instruction methods and materials for small-group learning.

From Lou, Y., Abrami, P. C., Spence, J. C., Poulsen, C., Chambers, B. & d'Apollonia, S. (1996). Within-class grouping: a meta-analysis. *Review of Educational Research*, 66, 423–58. Copyright (1996) by the American Educational Research Association; reproduced with permission from the publisher.

RESEARCH DESIGN AND POTENTIAL FOR PUBLICATION

You need to take great care when selecting a research design to answer your research questions. In short, at the final point of submitting your work for publication editors and reviewers will go through your design with a fine-tooth comb. Clearly in their sights will be the appropriateness of the design, the sample size used, your control of potentially confounding variables, and, finally, the appropriateness and robustness of the statistical or qualitative analyses used in your study. If any of these are flawed you will compromise the potential for your research to be published. You should consult good methodology books to ensure that your design is appropriate and robust before you invest time and energy in your project.

SUGGESTED READINGS

American Psychological Association (1994). *Publication manual of the American Psychological Association*, 4th edition. Washington, DC: American Psychological Association.

Banyard, P. & Grayson, A. (1996). *Introducing psychological research.* London: Macmillan.

Christensen, L. B. (1997). *Experimental methodology*, 7th edition. Needham Heights, MA: Allyn & Bacon.

Creswell, J. W. (1998). *Qualitative inquiry and research design. Choosing among five traditions.* Thousand Oaks, CA: Sage.

Denzin, N. K. & Lincoln, Y. S. (1994). *Handbook of qualitative research.* Thousand Oaks, CA: Sage.

Haslam, S. A. & McGarty, C. (1998). *Doing psychology. An introduction to research methodology and statistics.* Thousand Oaks, CA: Sage.

Huck, S. W. (2000). *Reading statistics and research*, 3rd edition. New York, NY: Longman.

Leach, J. (1991) *Running applied psychology experiments.* Milton Keynes: Open University Press.

Loos, F. (1995). *Research foundations for psychology and the behavioural sciences.* New York, NY: HarperCollins.

McBurney, D. H. (1998). *Research methods.* Pacific Grove, CA: Brooks/Cole.

Meyers, A. & Hansen, C. (1997). *Experimental psychology*, 4th edition. Pacific Grove, CA: Brooks/Cole.

Miles, M. B. & Huberman, A. M. (1994). *Qualitative data analysis: An expanded resource book.* Thousand Oaks, CA: Sage.

Pedhazur, E. J. & Schmelkin, L. (1991). *Measurement, design and analysis. An integrated approach.* Hillsdale, NJ: Lawrence Erlbaum.

Wadsworth, Y. (1997). *Do it yourself social research*, 2nd edition. Sydney: Allen & Unwin.

Whitley, B. E. (1996). *Principles of research in behavioural science.* Mountain View, CA: Mayfield.

Wolcott, H. F. (1994). *Transforming qualitative data. Description, analysis, and interpretation.* Thousand Oaks, CA: Sage.

3

SELECTING A JOURNAL OUTLET AND SUBMITTING YOUR ARTICLE

- Types and prestige of journals
- Styles of presentation—style guides and notes for contributors
- Typical formats of research articles
- Submitting your article

TYPES AND PRESTIGE OF JOURNALS

Types of journals

There is a wide variety of research journals in psychology, and a large number of other ones that publish psychological research (eg, journals in education and health). At the most basic level, many psychological journals are published in order to disseminate research in particular sub-areas of psychology. There are, for example, journals in personality and social psychology, developmental psychology, educational psychology, cross-cultural psychology, psychometrics, organisational and industrial psychology, behaviour therapy and neuroscience, social psychology, medical psychology, cognition, abnormal psychology, community psychology, consulting and clinical psychology, genetic psychology, learning and motivation, and so on! Some journals exclusively publish empirical and experimental research articles while others publish a mix of research articles, integrative literature reviews and brief reports. Some journals limit their scope to reviews or experimental studies, or qualitative studies. Some journals limit their scope to validation studies or quantitative studies. Again, if you want to be published you need to select a journal that best reflects the nature of your research or enquiry. If you submit a discussion article to an experimental research journal it will be rejected before review. One easy way to ascertain what journals publish is to read sample articles from a number of issues. This has the benefit of modelling the acceptable style for presentation of articles in particular journals. It is also useful to review the work of the Editorial Board and ad hoc reviewers of each journal, as these will form the core of reviewers for your work, and depending on philosophical, theoretical or methodological persuasions, a high quality piece may be rejected. This is not uncommon, and can be quite dispiriting and cause potentially good researchers to withdraw from research and publication.

Each journal publishes a set of notes for contributors that indicates the specific mission and breadth of the journal. These notes usually describe the nature of the research they will accept (eg, experimental, field studies, qualitative studies, meta-analyses, replication studies and validity studies), and the thematic area in which the journal specialises (eg, developmental issues, cross-cultural issues, meta-cognition, anxiety, sports psychology, social cognition, and any combination of these). Some journals, for example, publish experimental and qualitative studies over a wide field of psychology. Some journals also provide the opportunity for publishing briefer notes as well as longer studies. This latter opportunity is often very useful for beginning researchers as their research or early investigations are often more suitable for publication as research notes or developments on previously published research. You should take particular note of journals that allow this facility.

You need, therefore, to be very familiar with the mission statement of your proposed outlet so that you do not misdirect your manuscript. The following excerpt clearly presents the mission statement for the *Journal of Personality and Social Psychology*.

Journal of Personality and Social Psychology

The *Journal of Personality and Social Psychology* publishes original papers in all areas of personality and social psychology. It emphasizes empirical reports but may include specialized theoretical, methodological, and review papers. The journal is divided into three independently edited sections:

Attitudes and social cognition addresses those domains of social behavior in which cognition plays a major role, including the interface of cognition with overt behavior, affect, and motivation. Among topics covered are the formation, change, and utilization of attitudes, attributions, and stereotypes, person memory, self-regulation, and the origins and consequences of moods and emotions insofar as these interact with cognition. Of interest also is the influence of cognition and its various interfaces on significant social phenomena such as persuasion, communication, prejudice, social development, and cultural trends.

Interpersonal relations and group processes focuses on psychological and structural features of interaction in dyads and groups. Appropriate to this section are papers on the nature and dynamics of interactions and social relationships, including interpersonal attraction, communication, emotion, and relationship development, and on group and organizational processes such as social influence, group decision making and task performance, intergroup relations, and aggression, prosocial behavior and other types of social behavior.

Personality processes and individual differences encourages research on all aspects of personality psychology. This includes, for example, individual differences in behavior, affect, health, coping, and motivation. Articles in traditional areas such as personality development, assessment, structure, and basic processes are also appropriate. Applications of personality psychology to everyday behavior and applied psychology are welcome. Papers on the interplay of culture and personality are also encouraged.

The *Journal of Personality and Social Psychology* indicates that while it emphasises empirical reports, there is scope for publishing specialised theoretical, methodological and review papers. However, be warned, in these latter cases an author's work would need to be exceptional to be published in this high prestige journal. There is considerable detail in the notes outlining what the journal will publish. Potential authors should look at the key words (such as the interface of cognition, behaviour, affect, and motivation) used in the description and cross-reference these key words with their own article. If the proposed article does not line up in a clear way with these descriptors the article, irrespective of its quality, will not be accepted for publication. Again, I must emphasise that you need to align your work carefully with the chosen journal before you submit, otherwise it may be a waste of time and effort.

It is essential that you familiarise yourself with the particular mission of potential outlets for your research. As you will see from the excerpt below, an editor will automatically reject articles that do not conform to the specific purpose of the journal. It is also wise to browse in a range of journals in related areas as this will widen your horizons for publication.

From the Editor . . .
Basic and Applied Social Psychology

Over the years I have become increasingly concerned about the wasteful nature of the review process. The large number of journals and correspondingly large numbers of submitted papers put an enormous strain on the scholars called upon to serve the essential role of gatekeeper for the scientific literature. Using this resource ineffectively is a double tragedy. It impedes the review process through long delays and impedes science in general by taxing the schedules and patience of its talent pool. To help ease the strain, I will use a two-tier review process at *BASP*. I will serve as the initial screen for all submitted papers and will reject without further review those that are clearly inappropriate for the journal and those that contain such obvious methodological or conceptual flaws that seeking additional review would not increase the chances of publication. Papers that pass this initial screen will be sent out for review to members of the editorial board and other experts. This kind of system, of course, is used by most editors who view their jobs as more than glorified paper pushers. I will rely on it a bit more heavily perhaps than is typically the case in an effort to protect the time and talent of reviewers and to guarantee the highest quality of work published in the journal. By focussing reviewers' efforts a bit more, I hope to give carefully conducted research and carefully crafted papers the thoughtful attention they deserve by reviewers who can do a timely and constructive evaluation. One result, I hope, will be faster feedback to all authors.

Copyright Michael Strube, Editor, *Basic and Applied Social Psychology*.
Reprinted with permission.

I include below a rejection letter I received from one journal which effectively illustrates the points I make above.

Dear Dr McInerney,

I received the manuscript entitled 'Cross-cultural model testing: Inventory of School Motivation' which you submitted for consideration by *XXX*. I am sorry but I must decline to publish the manuscript. *XXX* does not publish studies that investigate narrow measurement questions such as the reliability or validity of a single instrument. Your manuscript would be more appropriate for a journal such as *Educational and Psychological Measurement* or the *Journal of Educational Measurement*.

I am returning two copies of the manuscript for your use in submitting elsewhere.

Thank you for considering *XXX*, and I wish you success in finding an outlet for your work.

I took the advice of the editor and submitted the article to *Educational and Psychological Measurement* where it was published some time later.

You can access most journals on the World Wide Web. These home pages usually include the notes for contributors and other details. You might also find the following two references helpful:

American Psychological Association. (1990). *Journals in Psychology: A Resource Listing for Authors* (3rd ed.). Washington, DC: Author.
Wang, A. Y. (1989). *Authors Guide to Journals in the Behavioral Sciences*. Hillsdale, NJ: Lawrence Erlbaum.

Prestige of journals

Not all journals are created equal! There is a pecking order in the rating of journals in psychology. Indeed, articles have been written on the varying status of journals in psychology (see, for example, Feingold, 1989; Howard, Cole & Maxwell, 1987; Institute for Scientific Information, 1998; Peery & Adams, 1981). A journal's rating reflects its circulation, its association with a particular organisation or publisher, the prestige of its editorial committee, the review process, the number of citations articles in the journal receive, whether it is indexed on major databases, and the degree of difficulty in getting published in that particular journal. Each of these is an important criterion.

Circulation

Major journals are usually associated with prestigious organisations such as the American Psychological Association, and as such, have a substantial credibility in the academic and research communities. These journals also have a wide circulation which reflects, but is not limited to, the very large membership of the association. There is also a wide range of publishers that produce many fine journals. The level of circulation of a journal is important as it influences the dissemination of the research findings. Obviously, it is important to have major discoveries or applications spread widely throughout the psychological community. Hence, there is a great desire by researchers to have their work published in journals with wide circulation.

Editorial committee and review process

The prestige of the editor and editorial committee also influences the status of a journal. The presumption is made that editorial committees made up of eminent researchers are more likely to vet articles stringently, and hence enhance the quality of the journal. Very important in this is the review process (which we discuss in detail later). Journals that provide blind reviews of proposed articles are generally regarded more highly than those that review un-blinded, and those that do not review. Many journals indicate that copies of articles are to be submitted without author identification so that a blind review may take place. Increasingly, a range of options on reviewing is being introduced, so that journals may include alternative review processes such as optional masked reviews.

Citations

A further consideration is whether the journal attracts significant citation interest. This refers to whether articles within the journal are cited frequently in other journals and research fora. This is a highly desirable characteristic as it increases the likelihood that research published within the journal will get wide exposure. It is also important that the journal is indexed and abstracted in databases so that the article can be easily accessed through searches. As you will note from the following, both the *Journal of Educational Psychology* and *Basic and Applied Social Psychology* indicate that they are indexed and abstracted.

Abstracting and Indexing Services Providing Coverage of the *Journal of Educational Psychology*

Academic Index
Biological Abstracts
Child Development Abstracts
Communication Abstracts
Current Index to Journals in Education
Education Index
Educational Administration Abstracts
Exceptional Child Education Resources
Index Medicus
Management Contents
PsycINFO
Research in Higher Education
Sage Family Studies Abstracts
Social Sciences Citation Index
Social Sciences Index
Studies on Women Abstracts

Basic and Applied Social Psychology (ISSN 0197–3533) is abstracted or indexed in: *Applied Social Sciences Index and Abstracts*; *IFI/Plenum: Mental Health Abstracts*; *Inventory of Marriage & Family Literature*; *PsycINFO/Psychological Abstracts*; *ISI: Current Contents/Social & Behavioral Sciences, Social Sciences Citation Index, Research Alert, Social Sci-Search, Focus On: Social and Personality Psychology*. Microfilm copies of this journal are available through UMI, Periodical Check-In, North Zeeb Road, P.O. Box 1346, Ann Arbor, MI 48106–1346.

STYLES OF PRESENTATION—STYLE GUIDES AND NOTES FOR CONTRIBUTORS

Each journal provides a set of style guides and notes for contributors. It is very important for you to pay careful attention to these requirements. Partly these requirements are in place to enhance the readability of each article, and partly to facilitate the publication process itself. In general, the style guides are brief and often refer the writer to the *Publication Manual* of the American Psychological Association (1994) with a comment such as: 'Authors should prepare manuscripts according to the *Publication Manual* of the American Psychological Association (4th ed.)'.

The *Publication Manual* provides a very thorough treatment of the content and organisation of a manuscript, expression of ideas, editorial style, and the publication process. You should purchase a copy of this manual to assist you with your writing. The following APA Style Essentials will give you a good overview of some of the basic requirements. It also provides Web addresses for examples. This document is available on the Web at http://view.vanguard.edu/psychology/apa.html and this address is hotlinked to other useful addresses.

APA Style Essentials

Douglas Degelman, Ph.D., and Martin Lorenzo Harris, Ph.D.
Vanguard University of Southern California

The *Publication Manual of the American Psychological Association* (4th ed., 1994) provides a comprehensive reference guide to writing using APA style, organization, and content. Students should plan on using the *Publication Manual* to answer detailed questions not answered by this 'APA Style Essentials' document. The purpose of this document is to provide a common core of elements of APA style that all members of a department can adopt as minimal standards for any assignment that specifies 'APA style'. Instructors will specify in writing when any of the following elements do not apply to a specific assignment that specifies 'APA style' (for example, when an abstract is not required). Instructors will also specify in writing when additional APA style elements must be observed.

Because of the nature of Web documents (needing to be displayed in a standard manner on different sized monitors at different resolutions on different computers using different Web browsers), this Web document is itself not a model of APA style. For an example of a complete article formatted according to APA style, go to http://www.vanguard.edu/psychology/psychapa.html. This link also provides the information necessary for you to view the 'PDF' documents used in this guide to show APA-formatted documents.

I. General Document Guidelines
  A. *Margins:* One inch on all sides (top, bottom, left, right).
  B. *Font Size and Type:* 12-pt. font (Times New Roman or Courier are acceptable typefaces).
  C. *Spacing:* Double-space throughout the paper, including the title page, abstract, body of the document, and references.
  D. *Alignment:* Flush left (creating uneven right margin).
  E. *Paragraph Indentation:* 5–7 spaces.
  F. *Pagination:* The page number appears one inch from the right edge of the paper on the first line of every page, beginning with the title page. (The only pages that are not numbered are pages of artwork.)
  G. *Manuscript Page Header:* The first two or three words of the paper title appear five spaces to the left of the page number on every page, beginning with the title page. [Manuscript page headers are used to identify manuscript pages during the editorial process.]
     [Note: Using most word processors, the manuscript page header and page number can be inserted into a 'header', which then automatically appears on all pages.]

II. Title Page
  A. *Pagination:* The Title Page is page 1.
  B. *Key Elements:* Paper title, author(s), and author(s) affiliation(s).
  C. *Article title:* Uppercase and lowercase letters, centered on the page.

D. *Author(s):* Uppercase and lowercase letters, centered on the line following the author(s).
E. *Institutional affiliation:* Uppercase and lowercase letters, centered on the line following the author(s).
F. *Running head:* The running head is typed flush left (all uppercase) following the words 'Running head:' on the line below the manuscript page header. It should not exceed 50 characters, including punctuation and spacing. [The running head is a short title that appears at the top of pages of published articles.]
G. *Examples of APA-formatted Title Page:* Go to http://www.vanguard.edu/psychology/titlepage.pdf.

III Abstract
The abstract is a one-paragraph, self-contained summary of the most important elements of the paper.
A. *Pagination:* The Abstract begins on a new page (page 2).
B. *Heading:* 'Abstract' (centered on the first line below the manuscript page header).
C. *Format:* The abstract (in 'block' format) begins on the line following the 'Abstract' heading. The abstract should not exceed 960 characters, including punctuation and spacing. The *Publication Manual* (1994, p. 10) suggests that abstracts of theoretical or review articles should have between 75 and 100 words; abstracts of empirical research articles should have between 100 and 120 words. All numbers in the abstract (except those beginning a sentence) should be typed as digits rather than words.
D. *Example of APA-formatted Abstract:* Go to http://www.vanguard.edu/psychology/abstract.pdf.

IV. Body
A. *Pagination:* The body of the paper begins on a new page (page 3). Subsections of the body of the paper do NOT begin on new pages.
B. *Title:* The title of the paper (in uppercase and lowercase letters) is centered on the first line below the manuscript page header.

C. *Introduction:* The introduction (which is not labeled) begins on the line following the paper title.
D. *Headings:* Headings are used to organize the document and reflect the relative importance of sections. For example, many empirical research articles utilize 'Method', 'Results', 'Discussion', and 'References' headings. In turn, the 'Method' section often has subheadings of 'Participants,' 'Apparatus,' and 'Procedure.' For an example of APA-formatted headings, go to http://www.vanguard.edu/psychology/headings.pdf.
  1. 'Main' headings (when the paper has either one or two levels of headings) use centered uppercase and lowercase letters (for example, 'Method,' 'Results,' 'Discussion,' and 'References').
  2. Subheadings (when the paper has two levels of headings) use flush left, underlined, uppercase and lowercase letters (for example, 'Participants,' 'Apparatus,' and 'Procedure' as subsections of the 'Method' section).

V. Text citations
Source material must be documented in the body of the paper by citing the author(s) and date(s) of the sources. The underlying principle here is that ideas and words of others must be formally acknowledged. The reader can obtain the full source citation from the list of references that follows the body of the paper.
A. When the names of the authors of a source are part of the formal structure of the sentence, the year of publication appears in parentheses following the identification of the authors. Consider the following example:

> Wirth and Mitchell (1994) found that although there was a reduction in insulin dosage over a period of two weeks in the treatment condition compared to the control condition, the difference was not statistically significant.

[Note: 'and' is used when multiple authors are identified as part of the formal structure of the sentence. Compare this to the example in the following section.]

B. When the authors of a source are NOT part of the formal structure of the sentence, both the authors and years of publication appear in parentheses, separated by semicolons. Consider the following example:

> Reviews of research on religion and health have concluded that at least some types of religious behaviors are related to higher levels of physical and mental health (Gartner, Larson, & Allen, 1991; Koenig, 1990; Levin & Vanderpool, 1991; Maton & Pargament, 1987; Paloma & Pendleton, 1991; Payne, Bergin, Bielema, & Jenkins, 1991).

[Note: '&' is used when multiple authors are identified in parenthetical material. Note also that when several sources are cited parenthetically, they are ordered alphabetically by first authors' surnames.]

C. When a source that has three, four, or five authors is cited, all authors are included the first time the source is cited. When that source is cited again, the first author's surname and 'et al.' are used. Consider the following example.

> Reviews of research on religion and health have concluded that at least some types of religious behaviors are related to higher levels of physical and mental health (Payne, Bergin, Bielema, & Jenkins, 1991).

> Payne et al. (1991) showed that . . .

D. When a source that has two authors is cited, both authors are included every time the source is cited.

E. When a source that has six or more authors is cited, the first author's surname and 'et al.' are used every time the source is cited (including the first time).

VI. Quotations
When a direct quotation is used, always include the author, year, and page number as part of the citation.

A. A quotation of fewer than 40 words should be enclosed in double quotation marks and should be incorporated into the formal structure of the sentence. Consider the following example:

> Patients receiving prayer had 'less congestive heart failure, required less diuretic and antibiotic therapy, had fewer episodes of pneumonia, had fewer cardiac arrests, and were less frequently intubated and ventilated' (Byrd, 1988, p. 829).

B A lengthier quotation of 40 or more words should appear (without quotation marks) apart from the surrounding text, in 'block' format, with each line indented five spaces from the left margin.

VII. References
A. *Pagination:* The References section begins on a new page.
B. *Heading:* 'References' (centered on the first line below the manuscript page header).
C. *Format:*
The references (with 'paragraph' indentation) begin on the line following the 'References' heading. Entries are organized alphabetically by surnames of first authors.

Most reference entries have three components:

1. Authors: Authors are listed in the same order as specified in the source, using surnames and initials. Commas separate all authors.
2. Year of Publication: In parentheses following authors, with a period following the closing parenthesis.
3. Source Reference: Includes title, journal, volume, pages (for journal article) or title, city of publication, publisher (for book).

D. *Example of APA-formatted References:* Go to http://www.vanguard.edu/psychology/references. pdf.

E. *Official APA 'Electronic Reference Formats' document:* Go to http://www.apa.org/journals/webref.html.

F. *Examples of sources*

1. Journal article

   Murzynski, J., & Degelman, D. (1996). Body language of women and judgments of vulnerability to sexual assault. Journal of Applied Social Psychology, 26, 1617–1626.

   [Note: Underline continuously from the beginning of the journal title through the comma following the volume number.]

2. Book

   Paloutzian, R. F. (1996). Invitation to the psychology of religion (2nd ed.). Boston: Allyn and Bacon.

3. Web document

   Degelman, D., & Harris, M. L. (2000). APA Style Essentials. Retrieved May 18, 2000 from the World Wide Web: http://www.vanguard.edu//psychology/apa.html

4. Document from electronic database

   Hien, D., & Honeyman, T. (2000). A closer look at the drug abuse-maternal aggression link. Journal of Interpersonal Violence, 15, 503–522. Retrieved May 20, 200 from ProQuest on-line database on the World Wide Web: http://www.umi.com/pqdauto

   [Note: Underline continuously from the beginning of the journal title through the comma following the volume number.]

5. Article or chapter in an edited book

   Shea, J. D. (1992). Religion and sexual adjustment. In J. F. Schumaker (Ed.). Religion and

Mental Health (pp. 70–84). New York: Oxford University Press.

VIII. Tables and Figures
The *Publication Manual* (1994, pp. 253–255) provides detailed instructions on the formatting of tables and figures. For an example of an APA-formatted table, go to http//www.vanguard.edu/psychology/table.pdf.

Journals may have special requirements such as the nature of the articles that will be considered for publication (we have already considered this issue), but also:

- their length;
- format, that is, typeface, font size, spacing, and printing quality (eg, all copies should be clear, readable, and on paper of good quality. A dot matrix or unusual typeface is acceptable only if it is clear and legible. Dittoed and mimeographed copies will not be considered);
- the presentation format appropriate for the journal (eg, authors should prepare manuscripts according to the *Publication Manual of the American Psychological Association* (4th Edition). Articles not prepared according to the guidelines will not be reviewed, and all copy must be double-spaced;
- how many copies are to be submitted (eg, six copies of manuscripts should be submitted);
- author details (eg, in addition to addresses and phone numbers, authors should supply electronic mail addresses and fax numbers, if available, for potential use by the editorial office and later by the production office);
- the process of review that will take place (eg, masked reviews are optional, and authors who wish masked reviews must specifically request them when submitting their manuscripts. Each copy of a manuscript to be mask reviewed should include a separate title page with authors' names and affiliations, and these should not appear anywhere else on the manuscript. Footnotes that identify the authors should be typed on a separate page. Authors should make every effort to see that the manuscript itself contains no clues to their identities);

- and where to send the manuscript (mail manuscripts to the appropriate section editor. Editors' addresses appear on the inside front cover of the journal).

Often journals will also indicate the nature of the abstract to be included (eg, all manuscripts must include an abstract containing a maximum of 960 characters and spaces [which is approximately 120 words] typed on a separate sheet of paper) and whether or not some keywords are to be included for indexing purposes (eg, authors should include on the title pages of their manuscript two to five keywords to identify the substance of their paper). Usually journals will also state that citations are to follow APA standards.

Many journals prohibit authors from submitting the same manuscript for concurrent consideration by other journals, and the publication of research that has already been published in other forms. You may be required to verify this in your letter to the editor or on forms accompanying acceptance of your article for publication. I talk more about this issue in Chapter 8. Authors may also be required to state in writing that they have complied with APA (or equivalent) ethical standards in the treatment of their sample, human or animal, or to describe the details of treatment. A copy of the APA Ethical Principles may be obtained by writing to the APA Ethics Office, 750 First Street, NE, Washington, DC 20002–4242. Statements of ethical standards may also be obtained from the Australian Psychological Society at The National Science Centre, 191 Royal Parade, Parkville, Victoria 3025, and from the British Psychological Society at St Andrew's House, 48 Princess Road East, Leicester LE1, 7DR, UK. Often journals will publish extended treatments of editorial criteria for submitted manuscripts and you should seek to locate these for the journals of your choice for publication.

TYPICAL FORMATS OF RESEARCH ARTICLES

Typically research articles in psychology have a predictable format. There is some debate over whether this 'typical' format is appropriate or whether it has acted as a straightjacket on research and its publication. It is not my purpose here to debate the merits of this typical format, but to describe it to you so that you may write your articles to enhance publication potential.

The typical format allows a clear explication of the study. The following parts are usually included in each article: Title page, abstract, introduction, method, results, discussion, acknowledgment, appendix (when included), and references. I will describe each of these briefly below and extend the treatment of key areas in subsequent chapters with examples. An alternative approach is presented by the *British Journal of Educational Psychology*, 1998, 68, 443–56.

Title page

The title page should include three main elements: the running head for publication, title, and author name and affiliation. The running head should be a meaningful abbreviated title. The title should indicate the nature of the study, and show good use of keywords that are used to index your article. Be careful that you are consistent in the personal name that you use for your articles. This is important when others are searching for your material. For example, I am listed on some databases as D. M. McInerney, Dennis McInerney and Dennis M McInerney. If a searcher puts any one of these into an author search, the other listings will not necessarily be located. I have learnt from this to always list my name as Dennis M McInerney for consistency. Your institutional affiliation should be the one relevant at the time the research was conducted. When the article is being blind reviewed, the title page will not have the author identifiers or institutional affiliations on copies sent to reviewers.

Running head: CHILDREN'S MOTIVATIONAL
BELIEFS ABOUT SUCCESS
Children's Motivational Beliefs about
Success in the Classroom:
Are There Cultural Differences?

Dennis M McInerney, John Hinkley, Martin Dowson
University of Western Sydney, Macarthur
Shawn Van Etten
University at Albany, State University of New York

Correspondence regarding this article can be directed to Dennis McInerney at University of Western Sydney, Macarthur, P.O. Box 555 Campbelltown, 2560 Sydney Australia or d.mcinerney@uws.edu.au

Abstract

The abstract of your research article is very important. It is the first point of contact of the reader with your work, and in it you should present an interesting (and very brief) summary of the research to entice the person to read further. It is also very important to do well because it is usually the part of the article that is indexed and abstracted on databases. Hence, if it gives an inadequate or faulty description of the project the potential reader might not read further. A good abstract may lead the reader to get the full article. The abstract of your article should be approximately 150 to 200 words long (journals will set their own limits for this). There are five main components of an abstract for empirical work. Each of these should be quite brief. They are: (1) a description of the area under investigation; (2) pertinent characteristics of the sample; (3) the method used including brief statistical information if relevant; (4) the findings; and (5) the conclusions, implications or applications.

Consider the following abstract to see how well it conforms to these components. You might like to number each component using the key above.

Abstract

Does being successful at school mean the same thing for all children? In Australia, research posits that Aboriginal Australian, Anglo Australian, and immigrant Australian children embrace different learning goals (i.e., mastery, performance, or social) according to their culture. In this study, a 38-item inventory was used to measure similarities and differences between Aboriginal ($n=496$), Anglo ($n = 1,173$), and immigrant ($n = 487$) Australian students' learning goal orientations. In contrast to existing conceptions, these findings indicate that the profiles of Aboriginal, Anglo, and immigrant students were remarkably similar, with students embracing a mastery orientation of academic success. Nevertheless, there were significant (albeit small) differences among the groups, and these differences indicated that Aboriginal students are more influenced by social goals.

From McInerney, D. M., Hinkley, J., Dowson, M. & Van Etten, S. (1998). Aboriginal, Anglo, and immigrant Australian students' motivational beliefs about personal academic success: are there cultural differences? *Journal of Educational Psychology*, 90, 621–29. Copyright (1998) by the American Psychological Association; reprinted with permission.

Other journals may stipulate different formats for the abstract. The British Psychological Society, for example, advocates a very structured format for their journals indicating that the abstract should be intelligible on its own without reference to the paper and should not exceed 250 words in total. The abstract for journals published under the auspices of the BPS should be structured using six required headings: Background, Aims, Sample(s), Methods, Results and Conclusions, with an optional Comment section. Of course these headings may need some adaptation in the case of theoretical papers and reviews. The point here is that you must look up the notes to contributors for your preferred journal to ensure that you have got the presentation right.

In the following sections I introduce each of the main components of a journal article which will be elaborated upon in later chapters.

Introduction

The beginning of the paper introduces the problem or area under study. It is usually not labelled. It develops the background to the problem or issue and, in particular, situates the study within the broader research context relevant to the issue. This context includes both material relevant to the substantive issue at hand, as well as material relating to research strategies that have potential or limitations for research on the topic. Some journals set quite short limits on the length of the introduction and authors are routinely asked to 'prune' the material. For this reason, the introduction should not be an historical treatment of the area, nor should it necessarily be exhaustive. It should be focused and selective and lead naturally to the research questions being addressed in the study. It is very important that the literature referred to is current. It is often useful to finish this section with the questions being specifically addressed in the research. I describe features of good literature reviews in more detail in Chapter 4.

Method

The method section outlines in detail how the study was conducted. This should be sufficiently detailed for the reader to ascertain how well the study addresses questions outlined in the introduction. One criterion for assessing how well this has been done is whether the study is replicable on the basis of the detail provided in the article. Replicability of studies and their results is very important to evaluate the validity and reliability of the study's findings. Details need to be provided on the participants, any apparatus or instruments used, the procedure of the experiment or study, and the analytic tools being used to examine the data. These principles apply whether the study is qualitative or quantitative. I describe features of the method in more detail in Chapter 5.

Results

The results section carefully summarises the data collected and the results of the analyses conducted. These analyses may be statistical or qualitative depending on the nature of the analytical tools used, and the research questions asked. There should be a clear link between the presentation of the results and the flow of the introduction and research questions. Appropriate tables and figures should be included to clarify the results. When your description of the results includes statistical material you must be particularly careful to include adequate detail. I describe some of the components of this in Chapter 6. When tables and figures are used there should be a clear link to the textual description of the results. It is very important to make quite explicit what the major findings of the study are. At times authors 'bury' these major results in a mass of less important material.

Discussion

The discussion draws the threads of the study together. It should briefly review the research issues and the results while interpreting these and drawing out inferences. The development of the discussion should be logical and well sequenced. Again, it should follow the flow of the introduction and the results sections. A reader should be easily able to reference points made in the discussion with the research questions you posed and analyses conducted. It is not appropriate to introduce new, unrelated material here, nor is it appropriate to extrapolate beyond what your data and findings allow you to say. In other words, be circumspect in how you interpret your results and how you apply them to other situations.

It is appropriate in the discussion to consider the limitations of your study and future directions for research. At times the reviewer or reader might consider that you should have addressed some of the limitations before conducting the study, or that you should complete further studies prior to having the present work published. In other words, some limitations can be seen as 'fatal flaws' which will prevent recommendation for publication until they are addressed. Furthermore, piecemeal publication of smaller studies instead of larger, integrated studies based on the same data set is sometimes frowned upon by editors and reviewers. I say this to caution you to think carefully before committing yourself, and to use some of the criteria above to ask the question: 'Is the research ready yet for publication?' Remember that one major criterion for publication is what contribution the work makes to new knowledge or the new application of knowledge. Your discussion gives you the opportunity to forcefully argue this. But do not overstate your case. I further examine essential elements of a good discussion section in Chapter 6.

Acknowledgments

It is usual to include an acknowledgment for assistance received in completing the research. This should include acknowledgment of any grants awarded to fund the project, assistance received from participants and organisations, assistance received from colleagues in reviewing drafts of the paper, and any assistance with running the project that is important but falls short of indicating a shared authorship status. An example of an appropriate acknowledgment is given below.

Acknowledgment

We wish to acknowledge the assistance of Charles Vien who assisted in data collection at the Ecole Secondaire, Uashkaikan, Quebec, and Karen Swisher and James Arviso who assisted in data collection at Window Rock High School, Arizona. We also wish to thank the anonymous reviewers whose comments helped improve the manuscript immeasurably. This study was supported, in part, with internal research grants awarded through the University of Western Sydney, Macarthur.

Appendixes

At times you will want or need to include more detail than is appropriate in the body of your article. This extra detail might include more information on procedures involved in the study to enhance replicability, the instruments or materials used in the study, a summary of the variables used or that are salient in the findings, an outline of response categories or checklists, an outline of the phases of the study, or tables with extra details such as item and factor loadings for factor analyses. Most journals have a severe limit on what can be included as an appendix and will assess the need to include the material in terms of its contribution to the reader's understanding of the study. In the following example, details are given of the procedure for reciprocal questioning as it enhances the ability of others to replicate the study.

Appendix

Metacognitive Strategy Training

1. Copies of generic question stems adapted from the work of King (1991, 1992, 1993) were distributed to all students at the start of their first tutorial.
2. The purpose of these question stems was explained in terms of their use in facilitating problem solving, and in helping students to clarify their understanding and take responsibility for some of their own learning.
3. Examples of how these questions might be written were provided by the instructor, that is, modeling of question completion in relation to computing content. The instructor proceeded to pose specific content-related questions using some of the question stems several times throughout a tutorial each week.
4. Explanations of how these questions were to be used was given to students in this way:
   • students should write one question using a prompt from the generic question stems at the end of each tutorial, and write an answer to it as well;
   • these questions and answers should then be shared by students with the members of their small groups, that is, to be read out and discussed;
   • in addition, one other question should be selected and completed for 'homework' in the Reflection section of the students' class folders.
5. At the end of the tutorial, in the last 10–15 minutes or so, the overhead transparency on which the four self-regulatory questions were written was projected and explained in the following way:

- the questions are to be copied into the Reflection section of the students' class folders;
- the questions are designed as part of a problem solving strategy to assist students in focusing on what they are, and are not, learning at particular times, and in planning a course of action with regard to any difficulties;
- at the start of each week's tutorial, students will share their answers to the self-regulatory questions with members of their small group first, then in discussion with the rest of the class.

The self-regulatory (metacognitive) questions were:

a. 'What did I learn this week in my computing class?' (monitoring)
b. 'With what did I have difficulty this week?' (monitoring)
c. 'What types of things can I do to deal with this difficulty?' (problem solving/planning)
d. 'What specific action(s) am I going to take this week to solve any difficulties?' (planning)

These should form the basis of a review of content preceding each week's tutorial input by the instructor.

From McInerney, V., McInerney, D. M. & Marsh, H. W. (1997). Effects of metacognitive strategy training within a cooperative group learning context on computer achievement and anxiety: an aptitude–treatment interaction study. *Journal of Educational Psychology*, 89, 696–95. Copyright (1997) by the American Psychological Association; reprinted with permission.

References

Finally, your article should have a complete list of references. These should be presented in the appropriate style. Reviewers will look for two things in your cited references. One, the references should show a good contemporary knowledge of the area. The research may be questioned if it appears that you have neglected key articles or issues. Remember that the reviewers are chosen for their expertise in the area of your study and hence will (or at least should) be keenly aware of key references and studies. Sometimes it happens that a key article was written by a reviewer. If you are hapless enough not to have cited it, this will be drawn to your attention!

Second, the cited references should be obviously and clearly relevant to your study. Sometimes authors use referencing for the simplistic reason of adding weight to their study when the references are only tangentially relevant. This is a serious fault and should be avoided. Make sure not to overwhelm the reviewer or reader with personal citations, as this will often call into question the value of the piece of research on the larger research stage.

SUBMITTING YOUR ARTICLE

From the very beginning of writing your research article, you should be mindful of the audience you are writing for and the specific formatting requirements of the particular journal you hope to submit it to. Having this knowledge up front will make it easier for you to get through some of the more tedious aspects of manuscript preparation and submission. I have indicated above that each journal specifies the types of articles they will publish in cognate areas. Before you begin writing for a particular journal, it is advisable to read a number of articles from earlier volumes to get a feel for the journal. In particular, the journal might publish notes from the editor indicating their personal preferences. In this case you should read these carefully for information about content preferences, stylistic preferences and so on. In many ways publishing a research article is as much an art as a science!

The editor of the *Journal of Personality and Social Psychology* indicates clearly some of the editor's preferences in publishing articles in the extract below.

Editorial

Like students querying, 'Will this be on the test?,' authors typically are eager to learn what a new editor will accept for publication. The answer is clear: The contribution to knowledge of a manuscript will be paramount. Will a manuscript advance the science of psychology in a substantial way? It is not that the shortcomings of a manuscript or the research methods will not weigh in this decision—they will, of course. But the positive contributions of a manuscript must be weighed against its faults. Central to the decision for publication will be whether a manuscript can substantively advance the field and not simply whether it adds an unassailable iota of information.

In evaluating the significance of manuscripts, several factors figure prominently. A major consideration is whether the research is theory driven. Another is that research with multiple methods and multiple studies is usually more definitive than research relying only on a single type of measure or on a single study. A related consideration is that a multiple-study manuscript in a programmatic series of studies by the author is often most compelling, especially when it demonstrates that the major findings are replicable. Underused methodologies such as longitudinal designs, laboratory experimentation, behavioral observation, and cross-cultural approaches are often capable of giving stronger answers to questions than is true of single-time self-report studies. When global self-report measures of self-attributes are collected at a single session, it is desirable that they be accompanied by additional types of data, such as biological measures, informant reports, or daily diaries of behavior. Finally, novel approaches and theories can sometimes offer important new insights. Thus, submissions containing these elements will have a distinct edge because they are more likely to substantially add to knowledge.

Ed Diener, Editor, *Journal of Personality and Social Psychology: Personality Processes and Individual Differences*; reprinted by permission of editor.

Manuscript submission

Each journal will also have a set of directions about how to submit an article. These might include:

- Author guarantee that the paper is original and not under review elsewhere—this is common practice among psychological journals.
- The recommended length of the manuscript. This will vary from journal to journal and whether you are writing a full article, or a brief report. But you need to be careful not to exceed the suggested word limit as an overly long article will be rejected without review. It is my experience that it is better

for novice writers/researchers to write shorter pieces in the first instance as they are more likely to be reviewed, and more easily revised when reviewer comments come back.

- Presentational details such as font, spacing, paper size and title page details. While these details may appear trivial, ignore them at your peril. It is common for manuscripts to be rejected out of hand because they do not conform to the appropriate standards of the journal.

- Details on reviewing and what should go in the cover letter to facilitate this, including the type of review preferred. Some journals are blind reviewed, some are open reviewed, and some offer a choice. It is unusual that a journal will allow the option of suggesting reviewers. While the journal might not state this, it is sometimes reasonable for authors to request that editors not send manuscripts to certain reviewers. This may be the case with mixed-method or cross-disciplinary research where judgements by particular reviewers might be 'clouded'.

- Details on submitting the final copy of an accepted manuscript. Journal authors might be asked to provide a computer diskette along with a hard copy of the paper. This is becoming common practice.

- Details on the publication process including reviewing proof copies (not all journals provide this opportunity), and the responsibility for copyright permission. It is standard practice that authors personally obtain copyright permission on any extended material drawn from other sources.

The following extract from *Culture and Psychology* gives one example of manuscript submission guidelines.

Manuscript submission

Culture & Psychology

The following are instructions on the mechanics of submitting to *Culture & Psychology*. To determine whether an MS is appropriate for submission, please read the Editorial Aims of *Culture & Psychology*. Submissions: The journal publishes exclusively in English. Papers must be original and not currently under review elsewhere. Normally articles will be up to 8000 words including endnotes and references. Notes or commentaries should not exceed 2500 words. Paper presentation: Papers must be typed, double-spaced (12 point font) throughout on one side of 8.5″–11″ paper and must include: (1) Title page (authors' postal and e-mail addresses and telephone and fax numbers); (2) Second page: abstract (100–150 words) and about six key words; (3) Main text: prepared according to the American Psychological Association *Publication Manual* (4th Edition), UK or US spelling. In quoted extracts with numbered lines referenced in the main text, each line is to be maximum one-half page width. Title and section headings are to be given in three weights, A, B, and C. Quotations over 40 words are to be displayed, indented, in the text; (4) Acknowledgements and endnotes; (5) References (according to APA *Publication Manual*, 4th Edition). Initial Submission: Send six full printouts of the paper and a copy on an IBM-compatible disk (format: MS-Word version 5.1 or higher), with a covering letter to the editor). The covering letter should indicate whether the author prefers the manuscript to be reviewed anonymously or openly. Authors may suggest three possible reviewers. Reviewing: MSs are screened first by the Editor and one Associate Editor for an initial acceptance decision. Those papers considered to fit the scope of the journal are further reviewed by three independent and internationally representative reviewers. If the paper is accepted, substantive commentaries upon the paper may be published simultaneously. Submitted MSs will not be returned to authors. Final Version of the MS: Upon acceptance, authors are asked to provide a computer diskette (Macintosh or IBM compatible) along with the final version of the paper. Authors are responsible for guaranteeing that the final hard copy and diskette versions of the MS are identical. Proofs and Reprints: Authors will see proofs before publication and are sent 25 off-prints plus one copy of the journal upon publication. Authors are responsible for obtaining copyright permission for reproducing any illustrations, tables, figures, or lengthy quotations. For more detailed information, contact the editor. Book Reviews: Send books and suggestions to [the editor] at the above address. Copyright: Before publication authors are requested to assign copyright to Sage Publications, subject to retaining their right to reuse the material in other publications written or edited by themselves and due to be published at least one year after initial publication in the journal.

When you submit your manuscript you should accompany it with a short letter. The following represents a sample letter.

Dr X
Editor, *Journal of Psychological Scepticism*
Address
Date

Dear Dr X

I am sending to you five copies of my manuscript entitled 'A quantitative study on the likelihood of getting my article published' for consideration by your editorial committee for publishing in the *Journal of Psychological Scepticism.*
    I believe that the article makes an original contribution to research in an area relevant to your journal. The material has not been published before and is not under review by any other journal.
    I look forward to your comments on the manuscript.

Yours sincerely

When there is a choice of blind review or not, you should clearly indicate which you would prefer. Of course, if you are opting for a blind review you should have the appropriate number of manuscripts without identification included with the package. It is also appropriate to indicate in this letter if the material in the article has been presented elsewhere. For example, it is common for authors to present their work first as a conference paper, and then a refined version of it as a published refereed paper in a journal. At times you will see a note at the end of an article which states that the paper was first presented at a conference as in the example below.

An abbreviated and earlier version of this analysis appeared in the 1996 Proceedings of the International Conference on the Learning Sciences, IL.

In the next chapter I deal in detail with the literature review as a component of a research article.

REFERENCES

Feingold, A. (1989). Assessment of journals in social science psychology. *American Psychologist*, 44, 961–4.

Howard, G. S., Cole, D. A. & Maxwell, S. E. (1987). Research productivity in psychology based on publication in the journals of the American Psychological Association. *American Psychologist*, 42, 975–86.

Institute for Scientific Information (1998). *JCR—Journal Citation Reports on Microfiche. Social Sciences Edition*. Philadelphia, PA: Institute for Scientific Information.

Peery, J. C. & Adams, G. R. (1981). Qualitative ratings of human development journals. *Human Development*, 24, 312–19.

4

WRITING YOUR LITERATURE REVIEW FOR AN EFFECTIVE ARTICLE

- The purpose and nature of the literature review
- Sources of information—literature searches—databases—other articles
- Integrating information
- Establishing the grounds for research questions—statement of purpose

As I indicated in Chapter 3, the beginning of a paper usually consists of a literature review that introduces the problem or area under study. This review develops the background to the problem or issue and, in particular, situates the study within the broader research context relevant to the issue. This context includes both material relevant to the substantive issue at hand, as well as material relating to research strategies that have potential or limitations for research on the topic. In this chapter I will examine the purpose and nature of literature reviews in some detail, so that you can read them for understanding and write reviews that are focused and selective, and lead naturally to the research questions being addressed in your study.

THE PURPOSE AND NATURE OF THE LITERATURE REVIEW

In order to design effective research, you need to complete an effective literature search and review prior to commencing your research. And in order to write effective research papers, you need to complete a thorough literature review. There is no short cut here. Among the purposes of a literature review are:

1. to establish the point of the study;
2. to establish what questions have already been asked about the area of interest and what questions remain to be asked;
3. to investigate how similar or related investigations were conducted;
4. to enquire whether there are theoretical models which help define the area of interest; and
5. to enquire whether there are established techniques or instruments that may be adapted for use.

You probably covered these when designing your original study, and the literature review for your article provides you with the opportunity to briefly outline what you found so that you clearly justify what was done and why. It is often common for the author to conclude this section of the paper with a statement of purpose for the research, or a series of research questions and issues.

Establishing the point of your study

Foremost in your introduction should be a clear explication of what you set out to study, and why. This statement should be brief and can occur at the beginning of your article or near the end of the literature review. The following illustrates how my co-authors and I explained briefly the purpose of our study in an article published in the *Journal of Educational Psychology*.

Thus, the focus of this article is to map out potential motivational differences among Aboriginal, Anglo, and immigrant Australian students and, in particular, the comparative salience of three achievement goal orientations: mastery, performance, and social goals. Do Aboriginal students, in contrast to Anglo and immigrant Australian students, embrace different goal orientations for themselves, and how do they perceive Anglo and immigrant students' goal orientations?

From McInerney, D. M., Hinkley, J., Dowson, M. & Van Etten, S. (1998). Aboriginal, Anglo, and immigrant Australian students' motivational beliefs about personal academic success: are there cultural differences? *Journal of Educational Psychology*, 90, 621–9. Copyright (1998) by the American Psychological Association; reprinted with permission.

What has already been researched?

While some research may be in completely new areas with little research history, it is more than likely that your research builds on and extends previous research. It is important for you to be familiar with this precursor research as it provides an effective framework for your study, and provides the reader with a context for your work. Your initial review should be exhaustive, although the writing up of it might well be very succinct. The review should deal comprehensively with related issues, and should mention key research and researchers upon which your work is built. It should not deal with, or get side tracked by tangential issues. The cited literature should include the most recent material available. You can assume that a reader of your article will already have some knowledge of the area. The knowledgeable reviewer of your work will not be impressed if you do not show an understanding of what has already been researched.

What questions have already been asked about the area of interest and what questions remain to be asked?

If you do not complete an effective review, you might be asking questions that have already been asked and, therefore, setting out on an investigation that will ultimately be fruitless in terms of making a contribution to new knowledge. A literature review should indicate the state of knowledge in the area by indicating briefly what has already been studied and the results provided by these studies. This then allows you to build upon this knowledge, by either asking new questions, extension questions, or placing the 'old' questions in a new context. For example, existing studies might have been conducted with particular samples and you might wish to see if the 'answers' apply to different samples or in different situations. Very often conflicting answers are produced by research, and your research might be directed towards clarifying the issue. It might also be that you wish to challenge existing 'answers' by pointing out the perceived flaws in earlier research. Your review enables you to clearly indicate what you perceive the present knowledge to be, and the questions you wish to ask to extend that knowledge. In the following excerpt, I indicate that I wish to build on a particular model of social motivation to extend knowledge in this area.

The present article intends to investigate this [earlier] use of the Triandis model further by subjecting the items developed on the basis of the model [the Behavioral Intentions Questionnaire] to exploratory factor analysis. Further, the article examines the usefulness of the derived factors in predicting students' intentions to complete schooling.

There are a number of reasons for testing the earlier raw score application of the Triandis model through exploratory factor analysis. First, the earlier analyses were based on raw scores derived from components making up the model. The components of the model appear to have face validity as separate variables, but it is necessary to examine if the components actually are separate variables. Factor analysis is a suitable method for studying the face validity of items designed to operationalize the model. Second, in the earlier analyses it was assumed that the components of the model were equally appropriate for each of the cultural groups studied (i.e., the components measured were etic in nature). Again, it is necessary to study this more closely, with factor analysis being an appropriate tool. Third, the use of raw scores in multiple regression analysis may miss some of the important dimensions of the statistics associated with the scores. With factor analysis we are able to derive factor scores which are a more powerful summation of the relationship between each of the variables in the analyses. Fourth, correlations may potentially exist between the predictor variables so that some of them may be redundant. In its data reduction capacity, factor analysis may be able to reduce the number of variables needed to be used in multiple regression analyses. Fifth, it is necessary to demonstrate that each perceived consequence and its valuation forms one dimension. In the raw score analysis it was assumed that each did. Last, semantic differential scales (good/bad, useful/useless, pleasant/unpleasant, and important/unimportant), based on Osgood, Miron, and May's (1975) research were used to evaluate the affect and perceived consequence components of the model. It is necessary to demonstrate that these scales do in fact measure the same dimension, namely evaluation. Factor analysis is an appropriate tool for this purpose (Gorsuch, 1983; Kerlinger & Pedhazur, 1973).

From McInerney, D. M. (1991). The Behavioral Intentions Questionnaire. An examination of face and etic validity in an educational setting. *Journal of Cross-cultural Psychology*, 22, 293–306. Copyright (1991) by Sage Publications, Inc. Reprinted by permission of Sage Publications, Inc.

How have similar or related investigations been conducted?

A review of the literature enables the researcher (and reader) to situate the research within the methodological context of other studies. From this part of the review should emerge key variables and methodological procedures that you either adopt, adapt or change. It might be, for example, that previous studies have addressed similar issues but were conducted using experimental or qualitative approaches while your study utilises a survey methodology. Because you are knowledgeable about alternative methods used by researchers, you can indicate the strengths and limitations of these approaches, and why the approach taken in your study provides an opportunity to explore the issue at hand in a novel way, with a possibility of extending knowledge. It is also possible that a methodology utilised in quite different re- search has application to the current study. Again, the review enables you to explain this. You might also indicate when instru- mentation used in earlier studies (such as questionnaires) is used unchanged or changed and the reasons for this. A long time ago I read an article examining the reasons why women from two countries, one predominantly Catholic and one predominantly Protestant, chose particular forms of birth control, or none at all [Davidson, Jaccard, Triandis, Morales, & Diaz-Guerrero (1976). Cross-cultural model testing: toward a solution of the etic–emic dilemma. *International Journal of Psychology*, 11, 1–3]. While this was not my research area it did give me methodological insights into how to conduct motivation studies in cross-cultural educa- tional settings. Indeed, I adapted both the methodolology and instrumentation for a series of studies comparing Australian Aboriginal motivation and Anglo Australian motivation in schools. The previous excerpt is drawn from this series of studies and illustrates how I built upon and modified the behavioural inten- tions model derived from this earlier birth control study.

What theoretical models are available that might help define the area of interest?

One reason for reviewing the literature is to ascertain what theoretical models are available that might help you determine how to examine specific research questions of interest to you. In most areas of psychological research there are complementary, contrasting and competing theoretical models used to explain human behaviour. There are theories of personality, theories of intelligence, theories of moral development, theories of learning, theories of organisational behaviour, theories of motivation, theories of sense of self, theories of development and so on. After much reading and reflection you will decide on a theoretical perspective that you believe is heuristic for the purposes of your study. Once you have decided on a perspective or perspectives, this will influence the design of your study in all its phases.· It is necessary, therefore, for you to indicate in your review the theoretical perspectives that inform your research. This feature can be somewhat problematic because it is not uncommon for research based upon one theoretical framework to be reviewed by a reviewer coming from a different perspective. This is one of the reasons why multiple reviewers are used to evaluate research articles. Irrespective of the potential for conflict over what is appropriate or not, as seen by your reviewers, it is essential for you to communicate clearly and unambiguously your theoretical sensitivities. In the following excerpt I illustrate how my co-authors and I introduced a section dealing with our theoretical perspectives.

Theoretical sensitivities

It is important to distinguish between two interpretations of goals found in the literature. Consistent with interpretations advanced by Dweck (1992) and Urdan and Maehr (1995), this article uses the term achievement goals to refer to a general orientation that directs students toward specific performance outcomes. This differs from the conceptualization commonly found in the literature (Zimmerman, Bandura, & Martinez-Pons, 1992), in which goals are more akin to specific outcomes. To avoid confounding these two conceptualizations, we use the term achievement goal orientation to distinguish this from *achievement outcomes* (see Urdan & Maehr, 1995, for a discussion on this point).

From McInerney, D. M., Hinkley, J., Dowson, M. & Van Etten, S. (1998). Aboriginal, Anglo, and immigrant Australian students' motivational beliefs about personal academic success: are there cultural differences? *Journal of Educational Psychology*, 90, 621–9. Copyright (1997) by the American Psychological Association; reprinted with permission.

This section of the article, then, further developed our understanding of learning goals, and social goals and Western and non-Western conceptions of these.

Are there established techniques or instruments that may be adapted for use?

A thorough review of the literature will also enable you to evaluate earlier methods and instruments and their relevance to your research. At times you might find the exact instrument or device you need, or a methodology that exactly suits your research. In this case, you need to reference your work to these earlier studies. There are good reasons for utilising existing instruments and designs. First, it reduces the proliferation of instruments and allows some further check of the validity and reliability of existing instrumentation. Second, there is some security for you in using well-tried designs, methods and instruments rather than launching out on your own. It is also not uncommon for researchers to borrow materials and methods from other studies and modify them. There are a number of reasons for this. You might want to improve the instrument or method; second, you might want to adapt an instrument or method for a different situation; third, you might want to condense or expand the instrument or method. When instruments or methods are developed from existing research, their precursors should be cited in your review. It is very important for you to make crystal clear why, and in what ways, you have modified the existing instruments or methods and the ways in which this has strengthened your study. I commonly make the following comment in articles using my Inventory of School Motivation.

The Inventory of School Motivation (ISM) used in this study was devised to reflect dimensions of Maehr's personal investment model (Maehr, 1984; Maehr & Braskamp, 1986) and to investigate the nature of school motivation in cross cultural settings (McInerney, 1988, 1992b; McInerney & Sinclair, 1991, 1992). The original 100 items in the ISM are based on items in the Inventory of Personal Investment (Maehr & Braskamp, 1986) rewritten to reflect an educational context.

In some circumstances a researcher might design completely new materials and approaches. This might be because nothing that exists will do the task effectively. To generate new materials and approaches is, of course, very important, and can be a major plus in contributing to the extension of knowledge. But in this case you must be very careful that your materials really provide something new and more effective than pre-existing materials and approaches. Again, you will not be in a position to judge this if you have not conducted an effective review of the research literature. In the case of designing new materials and approaches, you would indicate that while *x*, *y* and *z* approaches are used in other related research, they had significant limitations for purposes of your study. In the excerpt below, my co-authors and I introduce our article by indicating the perceived limitations in earlier measures of computer anxiety. We then further elaborate on the theoretical sources underpinning the constructs we operationalised in our research.

As Bandalos and Benson (1990) have pointed out, there has existed in the area of computer anxiety research for some time a degree of 'inconsistency in the hypothesized dimensionality of the construct, computer anxiety. If specific dimensions are hypothesized to underlie computer anxiety, a clear explication of these dimensions may allow for a more nearly precise measurement of this construct' (p. 51).
    The aims of the present study, therefore, were to design a scale that would clearly explicate these dimensions and that would measure, via valid and reliable scores, the multiple dimensions of computer anxiety in a

training situation for adult learners. These aims were achieved by incorporating into a model of computer anxiety for such learners a number of factors that had emerged reliably from previous anxiety research together with additional dimensions that were derived from theories of motivation and learning.

From McInerney, V., Marsh, H. W. & McInerney, D. M. (1999). The designing of the computer anxiety and learning measure (CALM): validation of scores on a multidimensional measure of anxiety and cognitions relating to adult learning of computing skills using structural equation modeling. *Educational and Psychological Measurement*, 59, 451–70. Copyright (1999) by Sage Publications, Inc. Reprinted by permission of Sage Publications, Inc.

SOURCES OF INFORMATION—LITERATURE SEARCHES—DATABASES—OTHER ARTICLES

Today there is no shortage of sources of information for your research. Not so long ago it was quite tedious to do a thorough search of the available relevant research literature. Now, the world of information is literally at your finger tips. The positive side of this is that literature searches can be conducted quickly and exhaustively. However, you need therefore to be aware that readers and reviewers will be less tolerant if the literature review is not thorough.

Typically, literature searches are conducted today using any number of computerised databases. Most of these are available through the World Wide Web. Common ones used in psychological research are PsychInfo, Psychlit, Sociofile, ERIC, Expanded Academic, Academic Research Library, IDEAL and Medline. Usually these provide you with an abstract of each article and you can make the decision to obtain a hard copy if the research appears particularly relevant. Some databases allow you to download the full text. Below is a sample printout from APA/PsycINFO. You can see the wealth of information that is provided. The subject headings are hotlinked to related articles and through a careful combining of searches you can locate many other useful articles.

Accession Number
Journal Article: 1998–11441–003.

Author McInerney, Dennis M. Hinkley, John. Dowson, Martin. Van Etten, Shawn.
Institution U Western Sydney, Faculty of Education, Research Degrees Div, Macarthur, NSW, Australia.
Title Aboriginal, Anglo, and immigrant Australian students' motivational beliefs about personal academic success: Are there cultural differences?
Source Journal of Educational Psychology. Vol 90(4), Dec 1998, 621–629.
ISSN 0022–0663
Language English
Abstract
Does being successful at school mean the same thing for all children? In Australia, research posits that Aboriginal Australian, Anglo Australian, and immigrant Australian children embrace different learning goals (i.e., mastery, performance, or social) according to their culture. In this study, a 38-item inventory was used to measure similarities and differences between Aboriginal ($n = 496$), Anglo ($n = 1 173$), and immigrant ($n = 487$) Australian students' learning goal orientations. In contrast to existing conceptions, these findings indicate that the profiles of Aboriginal, Anglo, and immigrant students were remarkably similar, with students embracing a mastery orientation of academic success. Nevertheless, there were significant (albeit small) differences among the groups, and these differences indicated that Aboriginal students are more influenced by social goals. (© 1999 APA/PsycINFO, all rights reserved)
Key Phrase Identifiers
motivational beliefs about personal academic success, Aboriginal vs Anglo vs immigrant Australian 7th–11th graders
Subject Headings
*Academic Achievement Motivation
*Racial and Ethnic Attitudes
*Racial and Ethnic Differences
*Student Attitudes
Australia
Ethnic Groups
High School Students
Immigration

Whites
Classification Code
Classroom Dynamics & Student Adjustment & Attitudes
[3560]
Population Group
Human; Male; Female. Adolescence (13–17 yrs)
Population Location
Australia
Form/Content Type
Empirical Study
Special Feature
References
Publication Type
Journal Article
Publication Year
1998
Update Code
19990101

It is also possible to access considerable information through a number of www search engines such as Yahoo, Lycos, Alta Vista and WEB Crawler. If you use these general search engines you need to target your search carefully so that you don't come up with useless sites. Nevertheless, I have found that by putting in appropriate descriptors I have discovered some very interesting, current and otherwise, difficult to obtain, information. There is also a large number of specific psychology websites to use to look for information related to psychological research. I have listed a number of these below. I have not looked at all these sites and cannot vouch for their quality, and no doubt many others could be added. I do know that APA, BPS, APS and PsychCrawler are particularly good sites. The beauty of using www sites is that they 'explode' through their hotlinks and provide you with a wealth of other sites to use for your reading, research and publication in psychology. It is probably a good strategy to start off with sites such as APA as these are more likely to be hot-linked to other quality psychology sites.

American Psychological Association
(http://www.apa.org/homepage.html

American Psychological Association Help Center (http://helping.apa.org/)

British Psychological Society (http://www.bps.org.uk/)

Australian Psychological Society (http://www.psychsociety.com.au/)

PsychCrawler: Indexing the Web for the Best in Psychology (http://www.psychcrawler.com/)

C.G. Jung, Analytical Psychology, and Culture (http://www.cgjung.com/cgjung/)

The Psychology of the Internet: Research & Theory Discussion List (http://www.cmhc.com/mlists/research/about.htm)

Psychology and religion

Psychology of Religion Pages (http://www.psywww.com/psyrelig/)

Psychology—Biographical methods

The Institute for Psychohistory (http://www.psychohistory.com/)

Psychology—Computer network resources—Directories

Catalyst: Information on Computers in Psychology (http://www.victoriapoint.com/catalyst.htm)

Psychology: University of California at San Diego (UCSD) (http://psy.ucsd.edu/)

Psychology, Pathological

Evolution (http://www.human-nature.com/darwin/index.html)

National Institute of Mental Health (NIMH) (http://www.nimh.nih.gov/)

Psychology—Periodicals

Annual Reviews in the Social Sciences (http://social.annualreviews.org/)

PsychNews International (PNI)
(http://www.mhnet.org/pni/)

Psychology, Religious

Psychology of Religion Pages
(http://www.psywww.com/psyrelig/)

Psychology, Religious—Study and teaching

Psychology of Religion Pages
(http://www.psywww.com/psyrelig/)

Psychology—Study and teaching—California—San Diego

Psychology: University of California at San Diego (UCSD) (http://psy.ucsd.edu/)

Social Psychology Network
(http://www.socialpsychology.org/)

Buros Institute of Mental Measurement
(http://www.unl.edu/buros/)

Psy Web (http://www.psywww.com/)

There are a growing number of electronic journals that can be accessed through the Web. The importance of using this source of information is that it is much more recent than hard-copy journals where there is often a considerable lag between the research being conducted and its publication. As mentioned earlier, an increasing number of traditionally print-based journals are now publishing electronically as well as in print.

List of descriptors

In order to conduct effective searches using these databases and Web sites you need to have a good list of descriptors which succinctly capture the content of your research interests. Once you have located one or two appropriate articles you can begin to build up your list of descriptors by including relevant ones from the published articles you have accessed. When you submit your article for publication you may be asked to include a set of descriptors for indexing, so it is very useful to become familiar with what are the most appropriate ones. As I mentioned before, the abstracted entry of your published article on a database may be the first point of contact of the reader with your work, hence it is important that you include appropriate descriptors.

INTEGRATING INFORMATION

Types of publication

There are basically three types of publication that will be of interest to you. First, you will want to access key empirical research articles related to your research. There is no substitute for your first-hand reading and synthesis of these. Second, particularly in well-researched areas, you will want to access key review articles that summarise the state of knowledge. These reviews will help you to identify the primary research sources that you will want to review first hand. Third, you will need to read theoretical papers and discussions that inform your methodology. These might include books, chapters in books, encyclopedias and monographs. If you are working consistently in an area then you will probably have some key theoretical references that you repeatedly refer to.

How much do you write and how many references do you cite?

Most journals have severe limits on space and so the literature review for your study will always have to be succinct, well focused, integrated and up-to-date. You can get a good feel for how much to write by considering examples of articles in the particular journals of interest to you. However, if you carefully synthesise information from reviewed journal articles it is quite possible to pack considerable information into a few lines. All key articles should be referenced in your review.

Many editors these days are asking authors to cut back on the never ending citation list—they seem to want authors to critically select references and not just list fifteen citations at the end of each paragraph. Hence you need to select your citations wisely, and make sure that they well represent the topic at hand. Furthermore, be careful of second hand citations as these can be inaccurate, and in any event are often coloured by the author's personal values and purposes in writing their article.

ESTABLISHING THE GROUNDS FOR RESEARCH QUESTIONS—STATEMENT OF PURPOSE

The literature review should have established the grounds for your research questions or hypotheses. Many articles, therefore, complete the introduction by stating the purpose of the research and, at times, provide a list of research issues that will be addressed in the study. I like this approach as it clearly relates the research to its antecedents, and provides a blueprint for the rest of the article. This is important because it provides the reader (and reviewer) with a means by which to evaluate whether or not the author was successful. In other words, unless the reader knows where the author is going, and why, it is not possible to evaluate whether the research findings, conclusions from these findings, or the presentation of these were successful. You will recall that, earlier, I quoted the statement of purpose of the research from

Thus, the focus of this article is to map out potential motivational differences among Aboriginal, Anglo, and immigrant Australian students and, in particular, the comparative salience of three achievement goal orientations: mastery, performance, and social goals. Do Aboriginal students, in contrast to Anglo and immigrant Australian students, embrace different goal orientations for themselves, and how do they perceive Anglo and immigrant students' goal orientations? We address these questions: (a) What is the salience of each goal orientation (i.e., mastery, performance, and social) for students' feeling successful at school; (b) how do students rate the salience of each goal orientation for other groups' school success; (c) what intra- and intercultural similarities and differences exist between students' perceptions of academic success for themselves and for other groups; and (d) how do individuals' goal orientations relate to school achievement criteria, and does this vary according to group membership?

an article my co-authors and I had published in the *Journal of Educational Psychology*. I repeat here this statement along with the research questions that guided the study.

At times the literature review ends with a series of hypotheses as in the following excerpt from an article on individualism and collectivism, self-concept and gender.

Hypotheses: The first set of hypotheses tested assessed whether there were differences in self-conception responses within each of the I and C groups while the following four sets of hypotheses tested for differences between I and C groups and Gender effects. In particular we predicted

There will be no differences within either (a) the four individualist or (b) the five collectivist samples in the frequency of reporting Idiocentric, Large Group, Small Group, Allocentric, and Evaluative self-descriptions. This prediction is based on the proposition that, if the I–C dimension is a meaningful explanatory construct for differentiating self-conceptions, there should be considerable agreement within both the I and C groups;

Respondents from the individualist cultures will give more Idiocentric and Evaluative but fewer Large Group, Small Group, and Allocentric self-descriptions than those from the collectivist cultures;

Respondents from the individualist cultures are more likely to give Large rather than Small Group self-descriptions. This trend will be reversed for the collectivist cultures. This prediction is based on the claim by Triandis (1989) that ingroups tend to be small in collectivist cultures but are likely to be large in individualist ones;

Male respondents from all nine samples will tend to provide more Idiocentric and Evaluative but fewer Large Group, Small Group, and Allocentric self-descriptions than the females;

Additionally there should be no culture by gender interactions in any of the above analyses.

In the next chapter I discuss elements of the method section.

5

WRITING YOUR METHOD FOR AN EFFECTIVE ARTICLE

- Reading and writing method sections for understanding
- Overview of research design
- Participants
- Instruments and procedures
- Procedures
- Analyses

READING AND WRITING METHOD SECTIONS FOR UNDERSTANDING

It is a common experience for readers of research to skim the method sections of research articles. Sometimes this is because the methods, instruments and statistical analyses used are quite familiar and so it is considered unnecessary to read the material closely. At other times the material is skimmed simply because the reader finds some of the material incomprehensible. There is an obligation on the part of the author to make the presentation of the method section clear and simple to facilitate the reader's understanding. There is also an obligation on the part of the reader to read the method material carefully to understand exactly how the research was conducted. It is a little futile to put any weight behind the results and their interpretation if you are not happy with elements of the research design and implementation. In this chapter, I discuss the method section of the article and make suggestions on how to make your writing clear and mean-

74

ingful to your reader. As a general principle it is better to include more than less in your method section and allow the editor the opportunity to prune unnecessary details. It is much easier to cut out sections than it is to add later, especially when lack of information results in an initial rejection of the article.

The outlay of the method section

In general, the method section of your article may consist of the following parts: overview of research design, participants, instruments and materials, procedure, and analyses. Each of these sections is usually labelled and should include sufficient detail for your study to be replicated. If you don't provide enough information, the reader will be left to wonder what you really did do. Many articles suffer from this flaw. On the other hand, you should not give unnecessary detail as this could distract the reader from the focus. Very complex studies, or studies that involve complex instrumentation may provide extra detail, and this may be included in an appendix. Alternatively, most articles provide an 'author's address' from which extra detail can be obtained. A note to this effect would be included in the article. There are alternatives to the format I present below, and in the next chapter on reporting results and discussion. You should review some top notch journals in your area of research to ascertain what alternatives are available.

OVERVIEW OF RESEARCH DESIGN

Typically the author of an article describes the design of the study. As I have indicated in Chapter 1, it is axiomatic that good research should be founded on appropriate design. A good research question will go nowhere without this foundation. The research strategies used by you must be clearly linked to the specific research questions and issues examined in your study. The nature of the data to be acquired to help answer these questions influences the method chosen to gain these data, and the type of analyses to be conducted.

Central, therefore, to the research design is the research issue. There are a number of methodologies designed for conducting psychological research. We have described these briefly in Chapter 2. To revise this for you, there are are experimental designs which attempt to truly control the experimental variables and seek for causal relationships; quasi-experimental designs which do not have the same level of control but also seek to examine cause and effect; and correlational research which is concerned with prediction and the association between variables. There is also a wide range of qualitative methods such as case studies, observational studies and ethnographies that are becoming increasingly popular in psychological research. And finally, there are integrative reviews and meta-analytic studies. Your task in this section of the paper is to succinctly describe the design of your study and to relate it clearly to your research questions. The reader should be able to relate each aspect of the design to the statement of purpose and research questions outlined in the introduction to the paper. In the situation that you are replicating a study or continuing work using established methods, the method section of a particular article might be brief with appropriate referencing to the other sources. This is also the case in research notes that need to be quite briefly presented.

Each of the designs for research mentioned above will have specific requirements for conducting valid and reliable research, and it is in this section that you describe how you addressed issues of validity, reliability and fidelity to treatment in your research approach. As this material is also closely related to the description of the analyses of the data, the two might flow into the one section. Alternatively, a description of the design might flow through each of the subsections of the Method. In the following, a study on male sexual arousal as elicited by film and fantasy, it was necessary to describe the method in some detail (which I will not repeat here)—it included the following design element.

> The test session involved eight paired film and fantasy segments. The sequence in which these eight sexual episodes were presented was counterbalanced across 32 subjects through four Latin squares, and an incomplete Latin square was employed for the remaining four men.
>
> *From* Koukoumas, E. & Over, R. (1997). Male sexual arousal elicited by film and fantasy matched in content. *Australian Journal of Psychology*, 49, 1–5. Copyright (1997) The Australian Psychological Society Ltd; reprinted by permission of the publisher.

PARTICIPANTS

Most psychological research includes humans (not all though, as there is flourishing research in animal psychology, and some studies, called meta-studies, analyse the data of a number of other earlier studies). In your article you must clearly and succinctly describe those features of your sample that are of interest in your analyses as experimental variables, or that need to be described because they are important for the interpretation of the results, or because of their potential confounding effects on the results. For example, if you compare two groups for the benefits of training in the reduction of anxiety, one receiving a particular treatment such as cognitive training, and one receiving no treatment, it is essential that the two groups are equivalent on specific characteristics before the study begins. It would confound the results if either group had characteristics, such as educational level, which differed from the other group. You must provide details on relevant characteristics in your description of the sample. For example, in an article examining the positive and negative affective response of trained and untrained subjects during and after aerobic exercise the author described the sample succinctly as:

> Trained male runners from a university track and cross-country team (n=13) and untrained age-matched males (n=14) were recruited to participate in a fitness evaluation study. Subject characteristics are presented in Table 1. (Table 1 presents means and standard deviations on age, height and weights.)
>
> *From* Boucher, S. H., McAuley, E. & Courneya, K. S. (1997). Positive and negative affective response of trained and untrained subjects during and after aerobic exercise. *Australian Journal of Psychology*, 49, 28–32. Copyright (1997) The Australian Psychological Society Ltd; reprinted by permission of the publisher.

It is also very important to describe your participants and sampling in qualitative research, particularly when the sampling was not a priori but emerged as the project developed.

Selecting your sample

When describing features of your participants, it is usual to indicate the number of participants included in each category. This is essential as certain statistical procedures require a minimum number of cases—significance levels are affected, and the generalisability of results are implicated. It is also important to indicate how the participants were recruited, for example were your participants randomly selected, were they volunteers or an entire available cohort? If you are describing experimental or quasi-experimental research it is important to report the procedures for selecting and assigning participants to treatments. The following description illustrates how this might be done effectively.

Participants. The participants were 20 female and male students from the First-Year Psychology course at the University of Sydney (mean age: 23.5 years; range: 18–38 years). Participants were assigned to the musically trained or untrained group according to their level of formal musical training, where trained participants were required to have had at least six years' formal musical training in music, either instrumental or vocal (mean: 9.9 years; SD=2.69), and untrained participants were required to have had less than two years' training (mean: 0.3; SD=0.68). A control experiment was conducted to eliminate any confound of musical training and general auditory perception as revealed in reaction time measures of intelligence (Stankov, 1988). The results on a simple reaction time task using single-tone and four-tone chord stimuli showed no significant difference between 22 musically trained and untrained listeners.

From Stevens, C. & Latimer, C. (1997). Music recognition: an illustrative application of a connectionist model. *Psychology of Music,* 25, 161–85. Reprinted with permission.

At times, you might reward the participants and you should indicate this. For example, in the earlier research on male sexual arousal, participants were paid and the authors made the following comment:

Potential subjects inspected the laboratory and were provided with information on test procedures before providing written consent for participation in the study. Although each subject was paid $20 on completion of the laboratory session, the contract allowed for the person to withdraw consent and terminate their involvement in the experiment at any time.

Generalising the results

It is also essential to provide sufficient detail on the participants for the reader to ascertain to which other groups or populations the results of your study might be generalised. I have provided a grid below for you to consider in the context of your particular study or studies. Which of the following characteristics are needed for analytic purposes (eg, as experimental variables), which are needed so that the validity of your research can be assessed by the reader, and which are needed to explore the potential for generalising your results?

	Purpose		
Variable	**statistical analysis**	**validity**	**generalisability**
Sex			
Age			
Socio-economic status			
Educational level			
Ethnicity			
Aptitudes			
Student			
Adult			
Professional status			
Employment status			
Health status			
Language usage			

It is really quite important in the design and data collection phases of your research to collect as much demographic information on your participants as possible. It is not uncommon for journal editors to require further information on participants, or to ask you to do extra analyses based upon some other grouping variables than the ones in your article, and unless you have the data you are stymied. In the aforementioned sexual arousal study, the selection criteria for the sample required participants to be between 19 and 30 years of age, exclusively heterosexual, not to have a history of sexual dysfunction or sexually transmitted disease, and not to have taken medication likely to affect capacity for penile erection three months prior to the study. Each of these criteria is specifically required in order to conduct a valid study using the stimuli outlined in the article. Editors and reviewers routinely comment that authors conduct studies in which there is not enough detail on the participants, or appropriate controls on the sample have not been included in the research design, or make generalisations, conclusions and interpretations that are not supported by the sample upon which the research was based. You must be careful not to make these errors.

Nonhuman subjects

The APA Manual (American Psychological Association, 1994) recommends that for animal subjects you report the genus, species and strain number or other specific identification, such as the name and location of the supplier and the stock designation. You should also give the number of animals and the animals' sex, age, weight and physiological condition. As with human research, you need to give full details on the treatment conditions so that the research may be replicated.

INSTRUMENTS AND PROCEDURES

Data are, of course, the raw material of the research. The researcher must decide what types of data are most relevant to answer their research question. Data may be scores on a test, reaction times to a stimulus, rankings on a performance, preferences and attitudes and observations. Given this, the researcher needs to decide how the data are to be obtained, quantified and analysed. The decisions made will influence the quality of the research and its validity. A research question being answered with poor data will founder. Your article must, therefore, effectively describe any instruments, equipment and procedures you used to obtain your data.

Surveys and questionnaires

Often in psychological research the main technique used is a survey or questionnaire consisting of items to which the participant makes a response. It is appropriate in your article to describe the nature of the survey instrument, its antecedents, and give exemplars of items used, unless it is a commonly used instrument with well-established validity and reliability. In the following excerpt, my co-authors and I indicate how we used a well-established instrument, the Adult Sources of Self-Esteem Inventory (ASSEI), to examine cultural dimensions of self-concept.

ASSEI is a 20-item inventory that requests each respondent to rate on a 1 (very low) to 10 (very high) scale the importance for him- or herself and his or her satisfaction with different aspects of a person's self-concept such as the physical, social, ethical, familial, and intellectual (see Appendices). For the Chinese, Indian, and Malaysian respondents each item was translated into the local language by teams of bilingual social scientists using the approved translation/back translation method (Brislin, 1986). In Nepal pilot studies showed that greater reliability was found with an English rather than Nepali version of ASSEI (English was the medium of instruction).

From Watkins, D., Adair, J., Akande, A., Cheng, C., Fleming, J., Ismail, M., Gerong, A. & McInerney, D. M. (1998). Cultural dimensions, gender, and the nature of self-concept: a fourteen country study. *International Journal of Psychology*, 33, 17–31.

If you make modifications to the well-established instrument these should be noted in your description. If your instrument is new, you might need to report some details on its validity and reliability at this point. Conversely, the reliability of a new instrument is often reported in the results section of an article. This is particularly the case if validating the instrument is a major focus of the research. In the next excerpt I describe the instrument used in the study on beliefs about success, cited earlier.

Instruments

In the two-part questionnaire, participants were asked, first, to think about times when they had felt personally pleased with themselves at school (eg, 'because you tried really hard to do better at your work,' 'because you set out to beat someone in a test, and did' and 'because you helped others with their schoolwork') and, second, to indicate what qualities they thought other students needed to be successful at school (eg, 'they are always trying to improve in their work,' 'they like to beat others at tests,' and 'they like to help others with their schoolwork'). There were 16 paired questions targeting mastery, performance, or social goal orientations (see Appendix B).

All items used a 3-point response scale indicating level of agreement, ranging from *no* (1) to *not sure* (2) to *yes* (3). A range of achievement data also were obtained, including the following: English and mathematics grades for the subsample of students completing their final compulsory year of schooling (Year 10), absenteeism, intention to complete schooling, and preferred occupation after leaving school. These variables were used as outcome measures in multiple regression analyses.

> From McInerney, D. M., Hinkley, J., Dowson, M. & Van Etten, S. (1998). Aboriginal, Anglo, and immigrant Australian students' motivational beliefs about personal academic success: are there cultural differences? *Journal of Educational Psychology*, 90, 621–9. Copyright (1998) by the American Psychological Association; reprinted with permission.

Physiological reactions

Your data might consist of physiological reactions to stimuli as was the case in the articles on music recognition and sexual arousal cited above. For example, the following excerpt from the music study shows how reaction time to stimuli were used as the data for analytic purposes.

> The reaction time data comprised measures of the time taken from the onset of the comparison sequence to the response 'same' or 'different' in the experimental trials. The data were converted into response latencies to give an indication of the amount of time that had elapsed from the point at which the first feature manipulation occurred in a modified sequence to subjects' responses.

> From Stevens, C. & Latimer, C. (1997). Music recognition: an illustrative application of a connectionist model. *Psychology of Music*, 25, 161–85. Reprinted with permission.

Observations

Your data may consist of observations and in this case you need to indicate the categories that you enumerated, and the schedule by which the observations were conducted. In the following excerpt, my co-author and I indicate how we conducted the observational studies as part of a research project.

Observational studies

Observational studies were conducted concurrently with the interviews described earlier. Two types of observational methods were used: structured classroom schedules and field notes.

Structured classroom schedules. Twenty-four (24) classroom schedules were completed in twelve (12) classes from which students participating in the interviews were drawn. Two observation periods (typically lasting between thirty and forty minutes) were completed for each class. The structured classroom schedules were developed, as the interviews progressed, to focus on key ideas identified in the interviews. This meant that each structured classroom schedule used a series of (up to eight) interview responses which acted as focus points for the observations.

The specific content of these observations focused on students' actual work avoidance behavior in various learning situations, and with respect to various learning tasks. These behaviors included students' conversations with each other (and, on occasion, with themselves) as they worked on specific tasks; any questions, answers, or other interactions students had with their teachers; and observations of the apparent intensity (or otherwise) with which students engaged in their work ie. whether they appeared distracted from, or focused on, academic tasks at hand and in what circumstances.

Field notes. Field notes were recorded concurrently with the interviews and classroom observations. The field notes were a more unstructured method of observation and were used in a more open-ended fashion. Thirty-seven field note entries were made. Entries in the field notes typically included notations concerning students' social and work avoidance behaviors and reactions to various learning situations, and the research processes themselves (eg, whether a student appeared to be comfortable and open in an interview or observation situation).

Special equipment

At times in experimental and other research some special equipment or materials may be used. These should be described in detail (sometimes in the appendix) so that the reader can visualise what took place, and other researchers can replicate the experiment or study. If the researcher was presenting visual or oral stimuli the nature of these should be described, including the number, order and any other relevant details. At times diagrams or photographs may be appropriate. Commonly used equipment such as stopwatches need only be referred to. In the following example, you will see how the authors summarised some of the special equipment they used in their study of male sexual arousal. I am including this example as it is somewhat more interesting than usual descriptions of equipment in psychological articles. But really, it provides an excellent example of appropriate detail in such a section, when it is warranted.

Equipment

Penile circumference was monitored throughout the session using a Parks Electronics mercury-in-rubber strain in the manner described by Julien and Over (1984). Changes in resistance of the gauge resulting from variation in penile tumescence were amplified by a Grass preamplifier (Model 7P1) and recorded on a Grass polygraph (Model 7). Paper speed was 5mm/sec for all records. The strain gauge was sterilised in activated gluteraldehyde (Cidex 7) before and after each use. Calibration permitting each man's responses to be expressed in millimetres of penile circumference was undertaken using the method described by Julien and Over (1984).

PROCEDURES

It is very important for you to describe in detail how your study was conducted. In many cases you will describe group testing procedures, in other cases, individual testing procedures. You need to describe in sufficient detail how the samples were organised, such as randomisation, counterbalancing, and other relevant features, as well as the experimental procedures used. At times authors also describe what was said to the participants to prepare them for their involvement. These features, together with those above describing the participants and materials, are given for two main reasons. First, so that readers understand clearly the way in which the research was conducted in order that they can make some assessment of its quality. Second, to provide other researchers with the necessary information needed to replicate the work, or to extend and improve it.

I include below details on the administration of a survey on comparative attitudes to health education of Catholic and Muslim students that I administered some time ago.

Administration

The survey, having been approved by the Department of Education and Training, School Committees, and the Human Ethics Research Committee at the University, was administered to students who had completed informed consent forms from themselves and their parents. The survey was administered by a team of researchers and assistants to either intact classes or groups of classes. Each item was read aloud in English while the students responded to it. To ensure confidentiality, the teachers were not involved in the administration procedures.

From McInerney, D. M., Davidson, N., Suliman, R. & Tremayne, B. (2000). Personal development, health and physical education in context: Muslim and Catholic perspectives. *Australian Journal of Education*, 44, 26–42. Copyright (2000) Australian Council for Educational Research Ltd. Reproduced by permission of the Australian Council for Educational Research Ltd.

ANALYSES

In many articles there is no separate analysis section and the analyses are reported under results. However, in articles which include an analysis section, you briefly describe key elements of your analytic approach. This might include a brief overview of the nature of your data, for example, whether your scores are nominal, ordinal, or ratio, or a combination. It should also include a brief overview of the parametric or non-parametric statistical techniques utilised and the reasons for this. These reasons should relate to their appropriateness to the particular research question being addressed, and to the nature of the data obtained. Some data can be analysed by both parametric and non-parametric approaches, some only by non-parametric approaches. Some statistical approaches are considered strong, others relatively weak. Some techniques are robust with small sample sizes, others need large sample sizes. Some techniques need an examination of the distribution of the data to ensure that it conforms to normal distribution parameters (the assumption of equality of variances), while other techniques may not need this. You will also consider your use of both descriptive and inferential statistics and their various purposes. You need to clearly justify, therefore, your approach in terms of the nature of your data, its strengths and limitations. It is not uncommon for editors of journals to reject articles because inappropriate statistical analyses were performed.

Analyses might also include qualitative approaches, and again, you need to describe what you did and why. In the following excerpt I include how my co-authors and I described the analyses performed in an article on self-concept.

Statistical Analyses

The items were coded such that higher scores reflected more favorable self-concepts. In preliminary analyses we examined the internal consistency of the domain-specific self-concept measures. Applying confirmatory factor analysis (CFA), we first examined the multidimensionality of the self-concept responses that has been widely supported in previous research. Then we examined the possibility of a higher order factor to represent the domain-specific self-concepts which in turn represent skill-specific self-concepts. The conduct of CFA has been described elsewhere (eg, Bollen, 1989; Byrne, 1989, 1998; Joreskog & Sorbom, 1993; Marsh, 1992, 1994; Pedhazur & Schmelkin, 1991) and is not further detailed here. In essence, CFA models were posited such that the designed items were allowed to load on the respective a priori factors only. Support for the multidimensionality of self-concepts requires a good fit of the multidimensional model to the data and correlations among factors to be reasonably low for each factor to be distinguishable from other factors. Support for a hierarchical representation requires the domain-specific factors to be correlated such that their relations can be explained by a higher order factor.

All analyses throughout this paper were conducted with the SPSS 6.1.3 version of PRELIS and LISREL 7 (Joreskog & Sorbom, 1988), using maximum likelihood estimation. The goodness of fit of models is evaluated based on suggestions of Marsh, Balla, and McDonald (1988) and Marsh, Balla, and Hau (1996) with an emphasis on the Tucker–Lewis index (TLI) which takes into account model parsimony, but we present also the chi-square test statistic and the relative noncentrality index (RNI). For an acceptable model fit (typically TLI > .9), for parallel items (with similar wording) correlated uniquenesses were included in the models a priori (Joreskog, 1979; Marsh, 1993b). All models reported here had correlated uniquenesses included for the parallel items. Whereas the goodness-of-fit indexes are useful in assessing model fit, it is also important to evaluate model fit on the basis of comparison between alternative models (typically by comparing their TLI values).

The CFA models presented here were based on a 40 × 40 covariance matrix (4 × 4 = 16 domain-specific and 4 × 6 = 24 subdomain self-concept items) with a sample of 249 for all models after listwise deletion of missing data. We first tested the hypothesis that there is a hierarchical relation among the domain-specific self-concepts so that they can be represented by a higher order factor. Then we tested further the hierarchical relation of a higher order Creative Arts factor with the domain-specific and skill-specific (subdomain) factors. Although we tested numerous alternative models, we report only the most critical models in two sections below (see Table 1).

You will note from this example that the statistical procedures used are relatively complex and therefore require some detailed description, although also note that we refer the reader to other articles and texts on the conduct of CFA so that we do not 'over dwell' on this issue. Even when the researcher uses more standard approaches, it is helpful to describe for the reader how and why they were used, as exemplified in the following excerpt.

Analyses

We conducted separate principal–components analyses on the 16 'success for others' and 'success for self' items for each of the three groups independently. As a quasi-confirmatory approach we set the analyses to extract three factors and examined the results in terms of the ability of the factors to define the targeted dimensions. The three extracted factors targeted were Mastery, Performance and Social goal orientations. We performed multivariate analyses of variance (MANOVAs), analysis of variance (ANOVAs), and paired *t* tests to consider differences between and within groups on answers to the two part questionnaire, and multiple regression analyses to examine the relationship between self-descriptions and academic achievement outcomes across the three groups in which the three goal orientations were entered as a single block. Because we believed that students' gender might interact with cultural group in influencing the main effects, we included gender as a factor in the MANOVA analyses. The categories of interest, therefore, were membership of a particular cultural group and gender.

From McInerney, D. M., Hinkley, J., Dowson, M. & Van Etten, S. (1998). Aboriginal, Anglo, and immigrant Australian students' motivational beliefs about personal academic success: are there cultural differences? *Journal of Educational Psychology*, 90, 621–9. Copyright (1998) by the American Psychological Association; reprinted with permission.

In the next chapter I consider the results and discussion sections in detail.

6

WRITING RESULTS AND DISCUSSIONS FOR AN EFFECTIVE ARTICLE

- Reading and writing research results for understanding
- Reporting results
- The discussion
- References
- Rereading your work

READING AND WRITING RESEARCH RESULTS FOR UNDERSTANDING

How often have you, as a reader, skimmed over the results section of a research article? Probably all of us do at some time or another. Among the reasons for this might be that the presentation of the results is unclear, confusing and overly complex. It might also be that we, as reader, do not have experience with, or expertise in, the procedures that led to the results, and therefore do not understand their presentation. In the first instance it is incumbent upon both the writer to write more clearly for his or her audience, and the journal editor to require revisions to make the presentation of results more readable. In the second instance, it is incumbent upon us, the reader, to familiarise ourselves with the procedures and analytic techniques used so that we can read with understanding the text, tables and figures that report the results. It is not very sensible to place any credibility in the discussion and interpretation of results if we have not scrutinised the results themselves for accuracy and validity.

This does not mean that we need to become methodological

or statistical experts in every procedure that might be used by a researcher. But it does mean that we should carefully connect the pieces of the article together to ensure they make sense to us—this means relating the results to the questions asked, the data obtained, and the analytic techniques used. We should scrutinise tables and figures to ensure they support the text presentation. We should also assess the significance of the substantive findings in terms of general criteria (such as levels of significance or confidence limits in quantitative research when appropriate), as well as common sense (related to issues such as size of sample, and substantive meaningfulness of any measurement differences).

REPORTING RESULTS

The results section is a very important part of your article as it tells the reader what you found out. Depending on the nature and complexity of your study, this can also present a problem in writing the results clearly so that the reader doesn't have to look for a headache tablet! There are three principles I consider important here in order to make your results section clear. The first of these is to revisit your research questions and to structure your results sequentially around these. The second principle is to clearly summarise each finding after its description. The third principle is to judiciously use tables and figures to visually summarise your results. I will look at each of these in greater detail below.

Research questions and results

My first principle is for you to revisit your research questions and to systematically structure your results around these. There should be a direct link between each reported result and a research issue—even when results are surprising or not statistically significant in quantitative research. You need to be very methodic about this. Underline and number, in your draft paper, each research question you intended to examine in your study. You might remember that I suggested that you end your literature review with a list of questions. If you have done this then the above exercise becomes easier. Then examine each result and number it against the research questions. You can address two issues as a result of this process. First, have you presented results for each of the research questions or issues indicated in your introduction? I have reviewed articles that refer to a number of research interests in the introduction but do not address them in the results.

Second, have you sequenced the presentation of your results so that they follow the flow of these research questions? It is not uncommon to find articles that present the results in a non-systematic way that is very confusing for the reader.

Summarise results

The second principle is to clearly summarise each finding after its description. This is particularly important if the results are somewhat involved (as many are). Your summary should be a brief statement that reminds the reader of the nature of the finding. Alternatively, the summary might be presented effectively in a table referenced to your text.

Once you have completed this process of numbering and summarising, which might appear to you to be rather uncreative and inflexible, you can review what you have written and 'soften the edges' of the approach as you see appropriate. Personally, I like reading articles that follow this tack as it makes it easier for me to keep the various details of the study in my head while I am reading.

Tables and figures

My third principle to enhance the readability of your results section is for you to judiciously use tables and figures. These tables and figures provide a visual aid summarising your findings. Tables can present exact values and can effectively present effects. Figures can be used effectively to illustrate comparisons and interactions. All tables and figures should relate explicitly to your text. Tables, figures and text should enhance the understanding of the reader by complementing each other—they should not simply repeat the same information in different forms and places. While it might seem overly obvious, you need to refer to every table and figure in your text. I also like it when the author takes time to explain the table in a clear way so that its contents are easily related to the text.

Tables and figures must be presented in the appropriate format. There are specific requirements regarding figure legends and numbers, guidelines on which are provided through the American Psychological Association *Publication Manual*. In general, tables and figures are presented at the end of the manuscript with a note like the following, 'Insert Table 1 about here', indicating where in the text the table or figure is to occur:

Each table and figure should be numbered sequentially in the order they are to appear in your article.

If you are reading a research article you should also be able to see all the connections mentioned above quite clearly. If you can't, then it is probably not a very well-written article. In reviewing a number of articles from this perspective, you will be sensitised to the advantages of approaching your results presentation in this particular manner. It is important to note here that you should not include interpretative comments or discussion in this part of your paper. These are left to the discussion section of the paper that I examine later in this chapter.

At times authors do present their results and discussion as one section. This may be because the results are limited and the paper relatively short. It might also be because the results, in and of themselves, either make very boring reading, or are somewhat convoluted or detached when separated from their substantive interpretation. I often find it difficult to read results and discussion sections of complex research papers, having to flip pages between the results and discussion to put the whole story together. One reason for keeping the two sections separate is to minimise the possibility that the reader will confuse the factual material (results) with the inferential material (the discussion). However, you might choose to combine the two. In this instance the reader should clearly be able to distinguish your interpretations from the findings.

Statistical presentation

If you are using standard statistical tests in your research you only need to refer to them by name. If you are using standard tests in non-standard ways, you should give your reasons for this. If you are using an unusual approach, or one that is unlikely to be familiar to your reader, you should include a description of the nature of the test and its purposes and strengths for use in your particular study. You should include appropriate descriptives such as means and standard deviations when presenting your results. When you are presenting the results of inferential statistics (eg, t tests, F tests, and chi-square), include information on the obtained magnitude or value of the test, the degrees of freedom, the probability level, and the direction of the effect. These can be included in either the text, or in companion tables.

Various manuals and guidelines for authors prepared by editors of particular journals list what they believe are the minimum details necessary when reporting inferential statistics (see, for example, Thompson, B. (1994). Guidelines for authors. *Educational and Psychological Measurement*, 54, 837–47). If you fall foul of these minimum details your article may be rejected, or at least, required to be revised. My co-authors and I have been through many rigorous review processes that have included both substantive reviews of the content of the article, as well as independent reviews of the statistical approaches we used (conducted by statistical experts co-opted by the editors). It is essential, therefore, that your statistical presentation conforms to the minimum guidelines and is presented in the appropriate format.

Given the fact that most journals are constrained for space, the results section has to be very succinct. You may need to be quite creative in your presentation of a minimum number of tables that include a maximum amount of information. In the following excerpt, the authors present the results of a quasi-experiment using two instructional approaches. Their study addresses the following two questions related to metacognitive strategy training and its impact on computer anxiety and achievement: (a) Is one instructional approach preferable to the other in terms of student learning, positive cognitions and anxiety? and (b) Are the two treatments differentially effective for high- and low-anxious students? The text was accompanied by tables summarising the statistical information. Consider how well the following, relatively brief results section conforms to the guidelines I give above.

Results

Preliminary two-group t tests were conducted to evaluate the equivalence of the two groups at pretest. There were statistically significant group differences ($p<.05$, two-tailed) on the prior competency self-rating scales, with the direct instruction group having significantly higher scores on three of the four self-rated competencies (DOS, word processing, and spreadsheet applications, but not databases). However, there were no statistically significant group differences on any of the pretest anxiety scales or positive cognition scales. Whereas there were some group differences in self-rated competency at the start of the study, these differences were controlled as part of the multiple regression approach to ANCOVA (i.e., self-rated pretest competency was used as a covariate in the analyses).

In Study 2 (see Tables 2 and 3), there were four

significant main effects and seven significant interaction effects at posttest. These effects are summarised in terms of three major categories of outcome variables: anxiety, positive cognitions, and achievement test scores.

Anxiety outcomes

There were significant ATI effects for five of the six anxiety scales, Learning, Competence, Equipment, Feedback, and Skills, all relating to aspects of learning and demonstrating computing skills (see Tables 2 and 3). In three of these interactions (Learning, Feedback, and Skills), students in the direct instruction group who were initially most anxious (i.e., with pretest mean scores of 4 and 5) experienced significantly decreased levels of anxiety ($p<.05$) at posttest compared with high-anxious students in the cooperative intervention group (see Table 2). In contrast, initially low-anxious students in the direct instruction group (i.e., with a pretest mean score of 1) experienced greater levels of anxiety at posttest than low-anxious students in the cooperative group. There were significant mean differences on the Learning, Competence, Feedback, and Skills scales (see Table 2). Hence, at least in terms of anxiety, high-anxious students tended to be more advantaged by direct instruction, whereas low-anxious students tended to be more advantaged by the cooperative intervention. There was, however, no significant main or interaction effect for the Fear scale (see Table 3).

Positive cognitions

Students in the cooperative group had significantly higher computing self-concept at posttest than students in the direct instruction group, and this difference did not interact with pretest self-concept (Table 3). There was a significant ATI for sense of control (Tables 2 and 3) such that students with initially low levels of sense of control were nonsignificantly ($.05<p>.10$) advantaged by being in the cooperative group, whereas students with initially high levels of positive cognitions did not differ significantly between the two groups.

Achievement outcomes

Students in the cooperative group had significantly higher achievement outcomes for the two folio assignments and for the research report but not for the practical computing test (Table 3). For the second folio assignment, there was an ATI. In follow-up analyses the largest differences occurred for cooperative group students with initially low self-ratings of computer competency (i.e., for pretest mean scores of 1 and 2). There were no statistically significant ATIs for any of the other achievement outcomes.

From McInerney, V., McInerney, D. M. & Marsh, H. W. (1997). Effects of metacognitive strategy training within a cooperative group learning context on computer achievement and anxiety: an aptitude–treatment interaction study. *Journal of Educational Psychology*, 89, 686–95. Copyright (1997) by the American Psychological Association; reprinted with permission.

THE DISCUSSION

At last you have completed your study, and have the results. The next step is quite exciting as you interpret these findings in the context of your research questions and background literature. The discussion gives you the opportunity to emphasise the theoretical relevance of the findings, or consider alternative interpretations of the findings and how plausible they are, or how further research may distinguish between your preferred interpretation and other possible interpretations. The discussion gives you the opportunity to consider consistencies and inconsistencies of your findings with other published research and any novel outcomes. The discussion is also the part of your article where you can extrapolate from your results and make generalisations and recommendations on the basis of your findings. It is important for you to subhead any material dealing with generalisations and applications that go beyond your data as this material will draw the close scrutiny of the editor and reviewers. Finally, the discussion allows you to comment on any limitations in your research that might affect the interpretation of the results, their generalisability, or that might be addressed in any replication study. However, you should not overemphasise limitations vis a vis the strengths of your research as this may jeopardise publication prospects. In the following excerpt you will see how authors of an article on dreams dealt with perceived limitations in their study.

Critics of this study should point to the one-source measurement of dream contents. Using dream diaries, we based our results solely on subjective reporting of dreams. Contemporary dream research relies on laboratory settings and physiological measurements of sleep and dream. The contents of dreams are recorded and thus accurately reflect a person's verbal expression patterns. The results of our study on the impact of violent environment conformed with results measured in laboratory settings among traumatized people (Lavie & Kaminer, 1991). Yet, gender, age, and cultural interactions may also reflect reporting patterns and construction of reality rather than accurate differences in dream content. However, our choice of using subjective written extraction of dreams may be justified, because spontaneous morning dream recall illustrates the cumulative effects of the night's dreaming and enables the generalization of the results in vivo situations (Stewart & Koulack, 1993). Yet, dream diary reports likely involved more elaboration, repression, and denial than did reports collected in a laboratory setting.

From Punamaki, R. & Joustie, M. (1998). The role of culture, violence, and personal factors affecting dream content. *Journal of Cross-Cultural Psychology*, 29, 320–42. Copyright Sage Publications, Inc. Reprinted by permission Sage Publications, Inc.

Again, as I suggested to you regarding the presentation of results, your presentation of the discussion needs to be systematic and structured around the research questions that formed the genesis of your study. Indeed, the discussion in many articles briefly reviews the research issues and findings prior to the interpretation and discussion occurring. It is appropriate once more to do some numbering. You have already numbered your research issues, and the results related to them. You should now attempt to interpret each result sequentially in terms of a research issue and make sure that you have a link between each research issue, a finding, and an interpretation. Some authors prefer to add a further element here and discuss their interpretation and make generalisations and so on. Other authors prefer to interpret each result systematically and leave a general discussion to the end. If the paper has been complex and involved a number of studies, it is often appropriate to include a summary and conclusion section (see, for example, McInerney, Roche, McInerney & Marsh, 1997).

Some people would not agree with my advice to structure your discussion sequentially in order of the initially stated research questions and results, and prefer to deal with what they perceive as the most important results first, and then to dispense with the less important or non-significant results. I do not like this latter approach because, at times, I think authors attempt to give the best 'spin' on their research findings while minimising or ignoring aspects that didn't work. Further, the important findings that are discussed sometimes aren't listed as research questions in the first instance. That new findings do not relate to research questions described earlier in the article is not a problem in itself, it becomes a problem when the research questions guiding the research are ignored.

I should also mention here that it is not uncommon for an article to present two or more studies. This reflects many editors' preference for such articles rather than piecemeal publication. In this instance the author may give a brief discussion after each study followed by a general discussion at the end of the article, drawing the threads of the research together.

REFERENCES

You should carefully read your manuscript to ensure that all cited references are presented in your reference list at the end of your article. It is not at all uncommon to find authors including references that are not cited, or citing references that are not included in the reference list. The checking of references is quite tedious (particularly if your article is long and cites many references) but it must be done. One technique that I have found useful is to tick each reference in the text and also in the reference list where it is located. This enables me to find references that are not listed. Any reference in my reference list that is not ticked at the end of my reading is not in my text and so is either introduced into the text as a citation, or deleted from the reference list. Of course, there are very specific guidelines on how to present references that are described in the APA manual. You must follow these guidelines (see also Chapter 3).

REREADING YOUR WORK

It is also important that you carefully proofread your work as sloppy presentation of the manuscript will count against you in the reviewers' eyes (if you are sloppy at presentation you might also be sloppy in research). Finally, and most importantly, you should have others critically review your work in draft form. This will enable you to address any inadequacies in the presentation and content of your research paper.

Hopefully, you have now written a paper that reports outstanding research and you submit it to a journal for consideration for publication. In the next chapter, I consider the review process and how to survive it!

7

THE REVIEW PROCESS 1

- Peer reviewing
- The review process from inside the journal
- Guidelines for review

PEER REVIEWING

One of the most terrifying elements of academic research publishing is the review process. Reviews are used by journals to evaluate the quality the research article. It is used as a vetting mechanism, and the process can be quite exhaustive (exhausting?) for the journal editors and reviewers, and for you, the author. There are various levels of review. There is the completely blind review, in which neither the identity of the writer or reviewers are revealed to each other. This is considered a very stringent form of review that alleviates claims of bias in the review process. *Child Development* indicates in the material below that it is a 'blind review' journal.

A system of blind reviewing is used at *Child Development*. It is the author's responsibility to remove information about the identity of author(s) and affiliation(s) from the manuscript; such information should appear on the cover sheet. The cover sheet will not be included when a manuscript is sent out for review.

Other journals implement an optional blind or open review process. In the instance of open review, the identity of the author is not anonymous although the identity of the reviewers may be. In *Culture and Psychology*, review may be open with both the author and reviewers' identity available and authors may suggest three possible reviewers.

> **Culture and Psychology**
>
> The covering letter should indicate whether the author prefers the manuscript to be reviewed anonymously or openly. Authors may suggest three possible reviewers.

Some journals have alternative forms of review, such as a dialogue between the reviewers and the author. In this case the identities of all parties are revealed. It is not my purpose to debate the merits of each form of review but you should be aware of the practice of the journals to which you are submitting your work.

Peer review, whether it is blind or open, is often the Achilles heel of many new researchers with one or two negative reviews of their research denting their confidence in both researching and publishing their research. In this chapter I hope to demystify elements of the review process and give you some handy hints on how to survive what is, more often than not, a very demanding exercise.

THE REVIEW PROCESS FROM INSIDE THE JOURNAL

What happens when you submit your manuscript to a journal for review? For most of us, the review process appears to be a black hole which sucks our intellectual efforts into it while we wait and wait and wait! Indeed, it is not unusual for authors to worry about whether their article was lost, accidentally forgotten by a journal editor, or so despicably bad that the editors/reviewers can't bring themselves to respond to it. However, these causes for the delay are very rare. The review process is lengthy, and depending on the area of the paper, and the availability of reviewers, it can take at least three months for a review to be completed. Indeed, in many cases it takes longer. I include the following e-mail correspondence I had with a very reputable journal about delays in a review on one of my articles. Names have been changed to protect the guilty! Remember, we are referring here to a review, not the publication of the article, which is a much more lengthy process.

Dr McInerney

We have received a copy of your ms and will be sending out written acknowledgment letter shortly.

Sincerely,
Joe Bloggs
Editorial Assistant.

About four months later I wrote:

Dear Joe,

I am enquiring about the status of the reviews on manuscript 99–04–202, which was submitted in April. Thank you for your assistance with this.

Regards,

Dennis McInerney

He replied:

Dr McInerney:

We've been having a heck of a time locating reviewers this summer. I have pulled your manuscript for the editors. Between the two of them they should be able to come up with reviewers.

Joe

I replied immediately:

Thank you Joe. This is an inordinately long period to wait for reviews given that the article was submitted in April. I hope the next stage will be expedited.

Regards,

Dennis

And he replied!

Dr McInerney:

Unfortunately, this is not a particularly long waiting period. We are still trying to locate reviewers for manuscripts submitted last Fall.

Joe

When your manuscript arrives at the editor's office it is usually given a log number which is used to track the manuscript through the review and publication process. After this the journal editor, or associate editor, reads the manuscript for an initial culling. At this point of the process, the editor assesses whether the article addresses the mission of the journal, makes a contribution to new knowledge or the application of knowledge, meets established ethical standards, and is presented in the correct format. Some journals have a very high rejection rate (greater than 70 per cent) and so it is at this stage that many articles are rejected. Articles can be rejected, or sent back to the author for correction, if they do not follow the appropriate guidelines for presentation, so as I said earlier it is very important to get these mechanical features of your article correct the first time round. It is worth pointing out here, and I will reiterate this in the next chapter, that just because an article is rejected does not mean that the research is poor, or indeed that the research article is poorly written. There are many reasons for rejection and you need to ascertain the reasons for rejection of a particular article. I know of authors who have gone through three or four journals before having a piece accepted, only to have the piece go on to become a seminal or well referenced article.

If the editor believes that the article satisfies the criteria for inclusion in the journal and is prepared in the correct fashion, they will send the article out for review. In this case a letter will be sent to you indicating this. Reviewers are selected from the editorial board of the journal, or from a list of ad hoc reviewers with expertise in the area of the research. This can often cause problems (and has for me) as the pool of reviewers for particular research areas can be quite small.

As I mentioned in an earlier chapter it is reasonable to request that your article not be sent out to specific reviewers if you are aware of potential bias on their part, or because of previous unsatisfactory experiences with particular reviewers (if you are aware of who they are). It is also reasonable that you request your article be sent to reviewers from relevant cognate research areas; sometimes articles are sent to reviewers from different disciplines or epistemological research bases to the ones in which articles are grounded. For example, in my research I often look at the sociocultural underpinnings of motivation. More often than not my work, although clearly psychological in orientation, is sent out to sociologists and anthropologists. And more often than not this causes me great problems as it is rare that researchers from these backgrounds appreciate my methodologies.

When selected, reviewers are sent a letter inviting them to review your article, along with a set of criteria for evaluating the research paper, and guidelines on how to prepare the report for the editor. In general, journals seek at least three reviews, and sometimes as many as five. The following presents an example of the type of letter editors send to reviewers inviting them to review papers.

Cover Letter

Enclosed is a manuscript that has been submitted to *Basic and Applied Social Psychology*. I hope that you will share your time and expertise by providing an evaluation of its suitability for publication. If you can help me, please read the enclosed reviewer guidelines and provide comments for the author(s) as well as your recommendation about publication. Your comments can be returned in the enclosed envelope, or you can FAX or e-mail your comments to speed up the review process. Please try to return your comments within a month of receiving the paper; I try to provide authors with editorial decisions within 45 days of manuscript submission so that their work is not delayed too long. If you are unable to review the paper within a month, please contact me immediately so that I can find another suitable reviewer (voice mail: 314–935–6545, e-mail: mjstrube@artsci.wustl.edu). I would greatly appreciate your suggestions for other qualified reviewers if you are unable to evaluate the paper at this time.

The review process would grind to a halt without the gracious efforts of experts like you. I know that completing a careful review is not a trivial addition to your schedule, so know that I truly appreciate your help.

Sincerely,

Michael J Strube
Editor

BASP web site:
http://www.artsci.wustl.edu/~mjstrube/basp.html

Reprinted with permission.

GUIDELINES FOR REVIEW

Each journal will send the reviewers a set of guidelines for reviewing a manuscript. The guidelines are based upon generally accepted principles for evaluating good research. Among the type of criteria that reviewers are asked to apply are:

• The paper contains one or more surprising results that nevertheless make sense in some theoretical context.
• The results in the paper are of major theoretical or practical significance.
• The ideas in the paper are new and exciting, perhaps presenting a new way of looking at an old problem.
• The interpretation of results is unambiguous.
• The paper integrates into a new, simpler framework, data that had previously required a complex, possibly unwieldy framework.
• The paper contains a major debunking of previously held ideas.
• The paper presents an experiment with a particularly clever paradigm or experimental manipulation.
• The findings or theory presented in the paper are general ones.

(From Sternberg, R. J. (1988). *The Psychologist's Companion: A Guide to Scientific Writing for Students and Researchers.* Cambridge: Cambridge University Press.)

A somewhat different set of criteria, taken from Isaac, S. and Michael, W. B. (1981) *Handbook of Research and Evaluation.* San Diego: CA. Edits Pub. are given on the table on pages 105–6.

Some journals indicate, in a general sense, how the reviewer is to report while other journals are more specific. The example on pages 107–9 illustrates this.

	Completely Incompetent 1	Poor 2	Mediocre 3	Good 4	Excellent 5
• The problem is clearly stated.					
• Hypotheses are clearly stated.					
• The problem is significant.					
• Assumptions are clearly stated.					
• Limitations of the study are stated.					
• Important terms are defined.					
• Relationships of the problem to previous research are made clear.					
• Research design is described fully.					
• Research design is appropriate for the solution of the problem.					
• Research design is free of specific weaknesses.					
• Population and sample are described.					
• Method of sampling is appropriate.					
• Data-gathering methods or procedures are described.					
• Data-gathering methods or procedures are appropriate to the solution of the problem.					
• Data-gathering methods or procedures are utilized correctly.					
• Validity and reliability of the evidence gathered are established.					

	Completely Incompetent	Poor	Mediocre	Good	Excellent
	1	2	3	4	5
• Appropriate methods are selected to analyze the data.					
• Methods utilized in analyzing the data are applied correctly.					
• Results of the analysis are presented clearly.					
• Conclusions are clearly stated.					
• Conclusions are substantiated by the evidence presented.					
• Generalizations are confined to the population from which the sample was drawn.					
• The report is clearly written.					
• The report is logically organized.					
• The tone of the report displays an unbiased, impartial scientific attitude.					

Basic and Applied Social Psychology

Instructions to Reviewers

As you may know, *Basic and Applied Social Psychology* publishes basic research in social psychology that can be applied to important social problems as well as direct applications of social psychological theory. We look to publish papers that are provocative and bring new perspectives to important social issues. Contributions to *BASP* are typically empirical reports, but we also consider theoretical, methodological, and review papers that address issues central to the application of theoretical social psychology. We seek papers that present a strong conceptual justification for the research, have clearly stated and carefully derived hypotheses, report appropriate methods and statistical analyses, and clearly discuss the conceptual and applied merits of the work. Your willingness to help us evaluate this paper along these dimensions is truly appreciated. Following are a few simple guidelines we would like you to follow:

Please return your evaluation by the date indicated on the enclosed rating sheet. You can speed up the review process by sending your review via e-mail or FAX. If you use e-mail, simply list at the end of your comments, the numbers (1–5 plus a percentile) that correspond to the judgments requested on the rating sheet. If you mail your review, send one copy; it is cheaper for us to make copies for the authors and other reviewers than for you to mail them.

Complete the rating sheet and provide detailed comments about the suitability of this paper for publication. The rating sheet will not be shown to the authors, so include on the back of that form any communication to the Editor that you do not want passed on to the authors. In your comments to the authors, try to be constructive. Try to explain clearly the rationale for your criticisms and concerns. Because a revision and resubmission may be encouraged, please be specific about the changes that you think are necessary to remedy the problems that you identify. Regardless of the publication decision, the authors can benefit greatly from your wisdom and willingness to share it.

Make a recommendation about publication on the rating sheet only. Reviewers are often selected because they have different areas of expertise relevant to the same paper. It is not unusual for them to disagree about publication because they may be approaching the paper from quite different perspectives. The Editor must take these multiple views into account along with his own evulation in rendering a decision about publication. In addition, the Editor must consider the page limits for the journal and so cannot publish all research that is merely technically competent. Authors sometimes have the misperception that editorial decisions are mere vote counts and so they get upset when the decision goes against popular sentiment. That problem can be avoided by indicating your opinion about publication only on the rating sheet.

Your identity will be kept anonymous unless you desire to reveal it. Don't put any identifying information on the review unless you want to make yourself known to the authors. This paper is a confidential communication. You should not show it to others, cite its content, or use it to further your own or others' work without permission. When you have finished with your evaluation, please destroy the paper to protect its confidentiality. If the paper is accepted for publication, you may request a preprint from the authors.

Thanks again for your help. I truly appreciate it. If you have comments or suggestions that you think would improve the review process at *Basic and Applied Social Psychology*, please let me know.

Michael J Strube, Editor
Basic and Applied Social Psychology
Department of Psychology, Box 1125
Washington University
One Brookings Drive
St. Louis, MO 63130

Phone and voice mail: 314–935–6545
FAX: 314–935–7588
E-mail: mjstrube@artsci.wustl.edu

Rating Form
Manuscript: S97–20
Reviewer: A
Please return by 6/18/97
Recommendation
Accept with minor or no revisions
Reject, but encourage to revise and resubmit
Reject, major problems not likely to be remedied in a revision
Evaluation
Check the most appropriate description for each manuscript feature.

	Fundamentally flawed	Major problems	Minimally adequate	Competently completed	Particularly creative or sophisticated
Description of relevant theory and research					
Derivation of hypotheses					
Quality of methods for testing hypotheses					
Quantitative analyses					
Discussion of results and implications					
Overall clarity of communication					

Compared to other published work in applied social psychology, how would you rank this manuscript in terms of potential impact (eg, likelihood of being cited by others, likelihood of influencing the direction of research in its area)? Provide a percentile score between 0 and 100 (100 = greatest impact):

Add any additional comments to the back of this form.

I have presented, earlier in the book, a number of rating sheets that might also be used by journal reviewers to rate your article. You should always have a mind to these guidelines while you are preparing your manuscript. It is also a good strategy to ask colleagues to review your article prior to submission using one or other of these guidelines. Please ask them to be honest as they may give a false impression in order to avoid disappointing you. I recall on one occasion being asked to act as a third author on a paper being presented to a very prestigious journal by a world authority in a particular area of psychological research. My job was to review the article and to add elements as I thought necessary. I read the article and was pretty much disappointed with it as I thought that it didn't meet a number of the elementary criteria for publication. I indicated this to the first author and indicated the changes that I thought should be made. The first author, nevertheless, ignored my advice and went ahead and submitted the article virtually unchanged. I was confirmed in my views when the article was rejected for publication, and the reviewers' comments reiterated what I had thought about the article. The moral from this is to take your peers' feedback and critique seriously if you wish to maximise your chances for publication.

When the review process is completed you will be sent a letter from the editor and you will once more be part of the loop!

RECOMMENDED READING

Sternberg, R. J. (1988). *The Psychologists Companion. A Guide to Scientific Writing for Students and Researchers*. Cambridge: Cambridge University Press.
Isaac, S. & Michael, W. B. (1981). *Handbook of Research and Evaluation*. San Diego, CA: Edits Pub.

8

THE REVIEW PROCESS 2—
RESPONDING TO
REVIEWERS' COMMENTS

- The review process from inside you
- The rejection letter
- The revise and resubmit letter
- Responding to the editor's and reviewers' comments
- Getting published

THE REVIEW PROCESS FROM INSIDE YOU

The first thing you receive from the journal is a confirmation that they have received your manuscript—this usually comes very quickly and will take something like the following form:

Dear Dr X:

We received your manuscript entitled: The Triumph of the Author over the Reviewer.
It was assigned the manuscript number: 298–1255
Your article was received in this office on: 15/12/00
and it was assigned to the editor: Joseph L. Doubting
Refer to the above manuscript number in correspondence about your paper. Note that it is APA policy that an article cannot be considered for publication if it is currently submitted to another journal. Also, the editor must be

informed if the data set(s) were used in other articles you wrote. We hope to get back to you within 75 days of receipt of your paper. You may use email to check on the progress of your paper if you do not hear from us in that time period. If the manuscript is accepted for publication, the copyright must be transferred to APA. Rejected manuscripts are not returned to authors unless this is specifically requested. If you are interested, The Journal has a web page on the internet; the address is listed above under the editor's return address. This web site contains the instructions sent to reviewers, as well as the rating scale used by reviewers. It also contains the editorial statement of the editor, the list of consulting editors, and a list of articles accepted for publication.

You may also receive a letter shortly afterwards from the editor that indicates that your article is not considered to be appropriate for the journal and will not be reviewed further. In this case there is no criticism of the research or article, but simply a judgement by the editor that it should be directed elsewhere.

Such a letter will go something like this:

Dear Dr McInerney,

I received the manuscript entitled 'Cross-cultural model testing: Inventory of School Motivation,' which you submitted for consideration by *XXX Journal*. I am sorry but I must decline to publish the manuscript. *XXX Journal* does not publish studies that investigate narrow measurement questions such as the reliability or validity of a single instrument. Your manuscript would be more appropriate for a journal such as *Educational and Psychological Measurement* or the *Journal of Educational Measurement*.

I am returning two copies of the manuscript for your use in submitting elsewhere.

Thank you for considering *XXX Journal*, and I wish you success in finding an outlet for your work.

Editor *XXX Journal*

THE REJECTION LETTER

If your article is accepted for review, at some point, usually when you have forgotten your article and when it is most inconvenient, you may receive one of three letters from an editor. The first letter, and one which everyone dreads receiving, is the rejection letter. The rejection may be based upon the editor's decision alone, or a consensus of the reviewers' and editor. In this letter the editor summarises the reviewers' comments and outlines the reasons for the non-acceptance of the manuscript. Usually the letter indicates that, even with revision, it is unlikely that the article will be publishable in their journal.

In general, the rejection letter is accompanied by the reviewers' comments so that you can ascertain the reasons for the rejection. Mind you, even with the reviewers' and editor's comments included it will sometimes be difficult for you to appreciate the reasons for the rejection. On other occasions, however, it will be crystal clear why your article failed to pass muster. The following represents a rejection letter I received from another journal. You will see from this letter how tough it is to get published in some journals, particularly when there is a clear disagreement between the reviewers over the publishable merit of the paper. In this latter instance of reviewer disagreement, editors often go with the rejection recommendation. I think this is because they think it is an easier way to deal with the problematic manuscripts, and in the back of their mind, always, is concern about the pressure on space in their journal.

Dear Dr McInerney:

Thank you for submitting your manuscript, 'Religious diversity and health education' to the Teaching, Learning, and Human Development section of the *XXX Journal*. Both editors and two expert reviewers have had an opportunity to read your manuscript and all agree that your manuscript addresses an issue of interest to our readership. However, the editors and reviewers are not in total agreement about the nature and extent of concerns the manuscript raises. Reviewer B was more supportive of the manuscript and suggests that a few minor revisions would make it publishable. Specifically, Reviewer B asks that you clarify the numbers in the sample. Reviewer B also suggests a title change that would be more consistent with the substance of the manuscript. Reviewer B also suggests you clarify your use of the term 'cross-cultural analysis'. The reviewer argues that rather than a cross-cultural analysis, you have an intra-group analysis of two religions.

Reviewer C felt that the manuscript lacked a clear purpose and did little to establish its theoretical or practical significance. This reviewer also felt that the manuscript had a number of open-ended statements that were unsupported by evidence. Reviewer C, like Reviewer B, commented on the confusion in sample numbers.

Based on these concerns and others detailed in the reviewers' comments (enclosed) we have decided not to accept your manuscript for publication in *XXX*. However, a rejection from this journal does not imply that your manuscript is unpublishable. *XXX* publishes a very small percentage of the manuscripts it receives. The reviews have provided you with excellent feedback that we hope you will find useful should you decide to revise the manuscript and submit it to another publication.

Thank you for considering *XXX*, and we wish you success in finding an outlet for your work.

Sincerely,
Editor, *XXX* Journal

There is little one can do at this point except accept the editor's decision. Some journals provide the opportunity for you to appeal the decision, although I personally think, unless an obvious error has been made, time is better spent revising the article for another journal. If an obvious error has been made it might be worthwhile to contact the editor by phone, email or letter to discuss this and to ask for a reconsideration. Don't treat the editors of journals as unapproachable, most are human and will appreciate your frank communication with them.

As I have suggested above, in most cases the rejection letter is accompanied by reviews that may be helpful in any further revision you might care to make of the article for submission elsewhere. You need to look carefully at the reasons for the rejection and decide whether, with revision, the article is worth pursuing in another outlet. It is my experience that every good article will get published, if not the first time round, at least on a second or third attempt. Do not take a rejection too much to heart. Many journals have very high rejection rates and you may need to try a different outlet. It might also be the case that the article was not really ready for publication and you can learn from the exercise. The important point here is not to be put off, but to use the experience positively. With regard to the above rejected article I had submitted, it was clear that there was a theoretical difference between myself and the reviewers, who apparently came from a sociological/anthropological background (surmised from comments and sources they indicated I should have consulted). In any event, the reviewers' comments were useful, at least to encourage me to be more clear in spelling out my theoretical perspectives. I submitted the article to another high level journal, and it was published (also with some revisions).

THE REVISE AND RESUBMIT LETTER

The acceptance with minor or no revision letter (very rare)

This is a letter that comes to the author all too infrequently! If you get such a letter, savour the moment, revise (if required), and then look forward to the next stages of the publication process. In the following letter, a number of important aspects are mentioned that form part of the publication process that you need to be aware of, including the assignment of copyright, supplying biographical information, and details on the proofreading processes employed by the journal. I will say a little more about each of these later in the chapter.

Dear Professor McInerney,

We are happy to inform you that your manuscript School Socialisation and the Goals of Schooling: What matters in Classrooms and Schools Characterised by Cultural Diversity has been accepted for publication in *The Clearing House*.

Please read and follow the enclosed instructions for submitting a diskette of your accepted manuscript.

Editorial changes to improve readability and to conform with our style and usage may be made here. We do not ordinarily submit proofs to authors. We will be in touch with you, however, if there are any copyediting problems or questions.

Please return the following to us in the enclosed postage-paid envelopes:

Assignment of copyright (one author must sign)
Biographical information sheet (one for each author)
Complimentary copy mailing labels (one for each author)
Reprints order (if desired)

To comply with copyright regulations, we need the signature of only one author, who will act as a representative for all authors on the assignment of copyright. Please return the form as soon as possible.

When the article is published, we will send each author two copies of the issue in which it appears. You may purchase additional copies at half the single-copy price. In addition, you may reproduce as many copies of your own article as you wish, using any copying method you choose.

You can order reprints by completing the enclosed reprint form and returning it in the envelope marked REPRINTS. If you wish to place bulk orders of the issue or to arrange for preprints, please call or write the managing editor,

Sincerely,
The Managing Editor

The rejection, but please revise and resubmit letter

It is a more common experience for authors to receive a letter from the editor which indicates that the article is not yet satisfactory for publication but may become so with appropriate revisions.

It is also common that editorial letters appear very negative in nature. During an editorial meeting of APA several years ago editors compared and contrasted response letters and decided that more informational feedback needed to be provided, and that many authors were even interpreting potential acceptances as rejections. You should carefully read feedback and understand that editors need to be cautious about leading on authors especially if there is any likelihood that the article will eventually be rejected. In the following excerpt I give an example of a revise and resubmit letter sent to me.

Dear Dr McInerney,

Enclosed are three reviews of your manuscript entitled 'Cultural perspectives on school motivation: the relevance and application of goal theory within individualist and collectivist societies.' Based on the reviews and our own reading of the manuscript we have decided against publishing the manuscript in its present form. However, we encourage you to revise and resubmit the manuscript. If you resubmit the manuscript to *XXX Journal*, we will read the revision to assess whether you have been sufficiently responsive to our concerns and those of the reviewers. If you have satisfactorily addressed our concerns, we will publish the paper without further review. If we have questions about the revisions made in response to the reviews we will ask the reviewers for their opinion and make a decision after reading their reviews. When you resubmit the manuscript, please include a cover letter describing your responses to the reviewers' and our concerns.

You need to read the reviews and consider all of the points made by the reviewers as you prepare your revision. However, in the remainder of this letter we want to summarise what we see as the most important issues and concerns.

The rest of the letter consisted of a succinct summary of the major issues the editor and reviewers wanted addressed in the revision. The letter was also accompanied by detailed reviewer comments.

It is at this point you, as author, have a major opportunity to work with the editor to revise the article so that it will be acceptable for publication. Yet it is often at this stage that the novice author gives up. There are a number of reasons for this. First, the letter from the editor may seem overly negative and pessimistic as to the chances of the article ever 'coming up to the mark'. Second, the apparent or real severity of the reviewers' comments may dissuade one from continuing with the exercise.

Third, the number of revisions required may be overly daunting. Fourth, these letters always arrive at the most inconvenient time when competing demands make the task of revision seem impossible. Fifth, the author is already tired of the project and wants to move on.

If you are serious about being published you must persist from this point—and this persistence will require great patience and diligence on your part. Even established researchers and authors are required to make revisions, and sometimes multiple revisions, before their articles are published. It is common practice in many journals to indicate the number of revisions at the end of the published article so you should look some up to see what I mean. I am not sure who holds the record for the most number of revisions on an article prior to publication, but the following one by myself and co-authors must come close.

Running Head: Hierarchical Academic Self-Concept

Where Is The Hierarchy Of Academic Self-Concept?
Alexander Seeshing Yeung,
University of Western Sydney, Macarthur
Hong-Sheung Chui,
Hang Seng School of Commerce, Hong Kong
Ivy Cheuk-yin Lau,
University of New South Wales
Dennis M. McInerney,
University of Western Sydney, Macarthur
Deirdre Russell-Bowie,
University of Western Sydney, Macarthur
Rosemary Suliman,
University of Western Sydney, Macarthur

18 September 1998
Revised 22 January 1999
Revised 6 April 1999
Revised 10 June 1999
Revised 30 August 1999
Revised 15 September 1999
Author Note

We thank all the teachers and students involved in this study, and Winnie Puiling Liu for helpful comments on earlier versions of this paper. Correspondence concerning this paper should be sent to Alexander S. Yeung, Faculty of Education, University of Western Sydney, Macarthur, NSW 2560, Australia. Electronic mail may be sent via Internet to a.yeung@uws.edu.au

Sometimes when you read the reviewers' comments you will be hurt by their apparent ferocity. I quote below from one particularly savage review I had from the *Journal of Cross-Cultural Psychology*. The reason I mention the journal on this occasion is to highlight for you the difficulty often inherent in writing up research that is cross-disciplinary, or which takes a different theoretical perspective to what is more 'normal' in that field of study.

The manuscript is extremely cryptic in its description of the central ideas and events of the study. For example, we never see a statement of what the Triandis Behavioral Intention Model is, and we are given scattered rather than systematic information about the contents and form of the BIQ. The presentation of methods takes up less than a page, and we are referred to other papers for the details. This strikes me as not a good idea. [*The reviewer then goes into a detailed critique of the theoretical framework and methodology of my study and concludes with the following*]

In sum, I think that the study is flawed by the most fundamental errors of understanding and a total lack of conceptual analysis. I cannot recommend publication, and I cannot see how it can be re-written to make it publishable. It is possible that the view I have taken results from the extremely cryptic presentation of methods and materials. If that is so, another try with much more careful elaboration of what was done might be worthwhile. But if I am correct about what was done, how it was dumped into the analysis, and what were the author's expectations for how it would come out, then the work is of no relevance at all.

After picking myself off the floor, I put the comments away and went on to another task. When my blood pressure had returned to normal, I reconsidered these comments and those of another reviewer which were more positive. I decided that my manuscript, not the research, was indeed flawed and hastily written. As the editor had given me an option to revise and resubmit I took seriously both reviewers' comments and revised the article. It was published later [McInerney, D. M. (1991). The behavioural intentions questionnaire. An examination of face and etic validity in an educational setting. *Journal of Cross-Cultural Psychology*, 22, 293–306], and you might like to refer to it to see how you can turn around articles and make them successful.

RESPONDING TO THE EDITOR'S AND REVIEWERS' COMMENTS

It is a good thing to receive an opportunity to revise your article for further review. It is a common experience by most authors that the revised article is enhanced by attending to the comments made by reviewers. Indeed, after we get over the shock of our work being evaluated, the reviewers' comments often make a good deal of sense. It is my belief that novice (and more seasoned) authors read many comments, criticisms and evaluations more negatively than they were intended by the reviewers, and that after a period of reflection, can work very positively on the basis of them. It is often a good idea at this point to share your reviews with some more expert researcher and writer, to glean from them what the real message in the critiques is, rather than what you have projected into them.

In responding to the editor's offer of a revision, there are a number of key elements that you must attend to. First, you must read the reviews very carefully, and cross-reference them with your text, annotating them with your views on the reviewer's comments. Second, distinguish between what are major theoretical or methodological issues (what might have been called by the reviewers limitations or flaws in the research), and more minor methodological, substantive or format issues. Often the letter from the editor will direct your attention to the major issues. Third, carefully work through which of the major issues you think you should and can attend to, and which ones you consider cannot be attended to (and whether these ultimately compromise the possibility of 'rescuing' the article). Fourth, work out a strategy for dealing with the most important issues. Sometimes this might mean major work such as a reanalysis or further analyses, the inclusion of extra material, or a refocusing of the study. Fifth, complete the required revisions in a very timely fashion. I try to turn around a revision in about a week. This indicates to the editor that you are serious about being published. It also avoids the problem that I once ran into where my revision took more time than expected and by the time I submitted it back to the journal, the editorial panel had changed! The revised article was then considered a new submission and went out to a fresh set of reviewers and was rejected!

When you have completed the revisions in the spirit of what was asked by the editor, it is essential to write a letter to the editor which specifies which revisions were attended to and how, and which revisions were not attended to. This letter needs to be very detailed and cross-referenced to your article and the reviewers' comments. I include an example below of my co-authors and my response to a very detailed critique of our article. You will note that we deal with each reviewer separately and specifically address the concern raised. You will also note that the reviewer comments address issues I have raised for your attention earlier in this book. You maximise your chances of a positive response by the editor if you go to this detail. I might also mention here that the article below is a long and complex one. You increase your chances, obviously, of having to do major and extensive revisions if your article is long and complex. My preference is for longer, substantial studies that hopefully make a major contribution to the research literature. However, I have to then be prepared to put more work into revising these longer articles.

Dear Professor X,

Thank you for your letter inviting a revision for the manuscript (99–XL–202R1) 'Where is the hierarchy of academic self-concept'. In the revision, we have addressed the comments and suggestions of the reviewers as follows:

Reviewer A
  1. *Refining the Introduction.* The reviewer would like to see the specific purpose of the study and how the four studies are related to that purpose at the beginning of the Introduction. In the revision, in the first paragraph (p. 3), we have added:

However, the hierarchical nature of academic self-concept is not as clear, leading to researchers' recommendation that the hierarchical aspect should be an important direction for further research (Hattie & Marsh, 1996). The present investigation comprises a series of four studies examining both the multidimensional and hierarchical aspects of academic self-concept. Studies 1 to 3 examine the structure of self-concept specific to a curriculum domain whereas Study 4 examines the structure of self-concepts in various domains in a school setting with a distinct curriculum focus. Overall, the purpose is to scrutinize both the multidimensional and hierarchical aspects of the Shavelson et al. model. In particular, the focus of the present investigation is on the possibility of an hierarchical representation of presumably multidimensional self-concept in specific subject domains and in an educational setting such as a school of commerce where the focus is distinct.

2. *More information in the Method section.* The reviewer commented that the Method section needed more information such as age range of participants, data collection procedures, etc. In the revision, we have added in more details in each of the four studies. Specifically, the Participants section for Study 1 (pages 9–10) now reads:

The participants were 298 students enrolled in a teacher education program in a university in Sydney, Australia (32 males and 266 females), ages ranging from 18 to 43. Creative arts are one of the key learning areas in the schools of the state and comprise a crucial component in the teacher education program. Consent to participate in the study was obtained from the students before they completed the survey. The data reported here are part of a larger study administered by trained research administrators.

The Participants section for Study 2 (page 13) now reads:

The participants in Study 2 were 197 ninth grade students of predominantly Arabic-speaking background (110 boys and 87 girls), ages ranging from 14 to 16 ($M = 14.49$), from three high schools in

Metropolitan Sydney, Australia. Most of the students spoke a LOTE at home (40% Arabic, 9% Vietnamese, 5% Greek, 4% Chinese, 1% Italian, and 14% other languages) and took a LOTE subject at school (61% studied Arabic, 9% French, 7% Korean, 6% Italian, 5% Greek, 3% Vietnamese, 1% Chinese, and 6% other languages). Permission to participate in the study was obtained from the students and their parents. Data collection was administered by a team of research administrators who read aloud each item in English while the participants responded to it.

For Study 2, in the Participants section (pages 17) we have added:

. . . the survey was administered by the class teacher.

3. *Statement on page 10.* We agree that the statement 'The data reported here are part of a larger study' was confusing. Essentially, the data reported in each of the four studies were part of a larger study. We have deleted this sentence in the revision.
4. *Negatively worded item.* Although the negatively worded item 'I'm hopeless in . . .' consistently reduced the internal consistency of each of the self-concept scales considered in all four studies, for most of the scales, the reduction in alpha estimates was not so serious as to warrant discarding the item. As reported on p. 29, even when the negative item was included, the reliability of each scale was still good (α .7). Our decision was to keep the Marsh (1992) ASDQ scales intact. The reviewer showed concern about this negatively worded item in the academic self-concept scale and asked why we continued to use it. Apparently, we did not spell out clearly enough in the previous version of the manuscript that we decided to discard this item for the academic self-concept scale but retain it for the domain-specific scales. In the revision, we have added on page 22:

For the domain-specific self-concept scales, the negative items did not seriously lower internal consistency and were therefore retained.

5. *Practical implications of results.* We have added on pages 25–26:

> With such understanding, teachers can feel more comfortable in designing self-concept enhancement programs with a focus on either academic self-concept in a more generic sense or specific self-concepts in more specific areas, or even in skill–specific subdomains, depending on the purpose.

Reviewer B

1. *More clearly spell out abstract.* The abstract has been revised to make it more clear to readers who are less knowledgeable in CFA.
2. *Criterion-referenced validity.* We agree that it would be nice to include criterion-referenced measures that could further test the validity of the higher order and global measures. In the revision, we have included this suggestion as a potential extension of the present investigation (p. 28).

> To provide even stronger support for the meaning of the higher order construct, a potential extension of the present study is to test the validity of the higher order factor. This can be done by relating it to an external criterion variable such as a general academic attitude measure (eg, Yeung & Lee, in press).

3. *Second paragraph.* The reviewer found that the second paragraph of p. 4 seemed to be out of place. In the revision, we have added a subheading, shortened the paragraph, and reorganized it (pages 3–4) so that it logically leads to the multidimensional and hierarchical issues.
4. *Explication of the I/E model.* Although relevant, because the Marsh (1986) I/E model is not the focus of the present investigation, we have chosen to delete the details but refer the reader to relevant references. Please also see Point 10 below.
5. *Description of Bong's (1998) study.* The reviewer commented that the description of Bong's study may not be relevant and could be misleading. We have deleted the paragraph completely.
6. *Self-perception constructs at lower levels of the hierarchy.*

The reviewer suggested that we discuss the potential similarities of skill–specific self-perceptions and self-efficacy. In the revision, we have added on pages 26–27:

> Even though the present investigation found support for hierarchical relations of self-concepts either in a focused curriculum or at a domain-specific level, it is also necessary to note that the hierarchy could be weak even in presumably closely related curriculum areas. For example, Study 2 found that students' self-concepts in English and in LOTE were only moderately correlated (r between the global measures was .24); and the correlation between the corresponding higher order factors derived from subdomain self-perceptions was even negative (-.13). The inconsistent pattern of correlations between the global English and LOTE measures and between the higher order measures derived from self-perception items showed not only that self-concepts in different languages cannot be assumed to be subsumed under a single Verbal construct, but also implies that the self-concept measures for English and LOTE may not represent the underlying constructs of the self-perception items. Because the self-perception responses in Study 2 are more like self-efficacy than self-concept items in that they do not necessarily involve affects and social comparison as typically found in self-concept responses (see Bong, 1998; Lent, Brown, & Gore, 1997; Lopez & Lent, 1992; Zimmerman, 1995), the skill-specific perception items in Study 2 can be taken as self-efficacy responses. From this perspective, then, the higher order factors derived from these responses may be taken as higher order self-efficacy constructs. Thus, on the one hand, the significant correlations between the higher order self-efficacy constructs and the global measures of self-concept in corresponding language areas suggest a noteworthy positive relation between self-concept and self-efficacy. On the other hand, the inconsistent pattern of correlations between the self-concept measures and between the self-efficacy measures for the two language areas (.24 vs. -.13) calls for further investigation of the relations between the self-concept and self-efficacy constructs.

This inconsistent pattern of correlations also calls for perhaps further investigation of potential implications for students' self-concept development described in the Marsh (1986) I/E theory.

7. *Details of participants in Study 2.* Please see Point 2 for Reviewer A above.
8. *Items for academic and skill-specific self-concepts in Study 2.* On page 13 of the revision, we have more clearly described the items:

   Skill-specific self-perceptions. Speaking, reading, and writing self-perceptions were each inferred from three items strictly parallel across the three skill areas. For example, the questions for reading self-perceptions in English were: 'How confident are you when you read English?', 'How well do you read English?', and 'How often do you read in English?' The corresponding questions for LOTE were: 'How confident are you when you read LOTE?', 'How well do you read LOTE?', and 'How often do you read in LOTE?'

9. *Incompatible results in Study 2.* We have more thoroughly discussed the results of Study 2 that did not show a pattern consistent with the other studies. Please see Point 6 for Reviewer B above.
10. *Further discussion of results.* We address this point together with Point 4 above. The reviewer asked for further discussion of results that might lead to alternative interpretations and perhaps directions for further research. In Point 4 above and in Point 10 here, the reviewer suggested that the predictions and assumptions of the Marsh (1986) I/E model be more clearly described, and the different patterns of correlations found in our Studies 3 and 4 be more thoroughly discussed in terms of this I/E theory or delete descriptions of the I/E theory altogether. Although the I/E theory is relevant, it is not our focus here. Thus further discussion in terms of the I/E theory may detract from our focus. Given that the different patterns of correlations between constructs within the English subject and between constructs in a highly focused school setting do not undermine our hypotheses and interpretation of findings, we have

chosen to (a) cut the description of the I/E theory but (b) add in the Discussion (pages 26–27) potential directions for further research based on these differential patterns (please see Point 6 for Reviewer B above).

Finally, we thank the reviewers for their very constructive comments that have hopefully helped to improve our MS. Enclosed please find four copies of the revised manuscript. Looking forward to hearing from you soon.

Yours truly,

Even after this extensive review the same paper went through a number of further revisions including formatting and statistical revisions. The following letter is a further one in this sequence of reviews and revisions.

Dear Professor X,

I write to submit a further revision of the manuscript 'Where is the hierarchy of academic self-concept' (99–XL– 202R1). In response to your penned comments on the previous version of the manuscript, in this revised version we have:

(a) cut back the introduction by over 2 pages,
(b) cut the discussion by 50%,
(c) moved a whole paragraph from the discussion to the introduction so as to provide a clearer account for the conceptual importance of the paper,
(d) edited the tables so that now they take about 40% of the space taken by the original,
(e) changed the sentences with semantical concerns,
(f) used LOTE as an acronym for language other than English in a singular form,
(g) added the issue of generalizability as a limitation in the discussion,
(h) deleted misleading/unclear statements (eg, lines 3 to 5 on p. 24 of previous version),

> (i) organized the text so as to improve its flow while retaining the points required by the previous reviewers.
>
> Enclosed please find four copies of the revised manuscript. Looking forward to hearing from you again.
>
> Yours truly,

As you can see from the above, the revision process is quite exacting and you must be very careful to address the editor's and reviewers' concerns. Even with a careful revision you are not guaranteed publication. Nevertheless, the effort is not wasted as the article, by-and-large, is improved and should see printer's ink in one form or another—hopefully in the journal of your first choice.

GETTING PUBLISHED

Once the article has been revised the editor renders a decision on whether it will be published. In most cases articles that have been revised well are accepted and you will be asked to sign a copyright agreement. The nature of this agreement varies from journal to journal. In general, copyright conditions may provide the publisher with sole control of the manuscript for future publication purposes, or may provide the author with the right to publish all or part of the work in books or articles he or she might write or edit in the future. The agreement will also require you to warrant that the work is solely yours (and your co-authors).

From this point you will be contacted by the publisher regarding checking a copy-edited manuscript which may include editorial alterations to the text to correct errors, make the text more readable, or to rationalise aspects of the text to fit publication parameters. Some journals then send proof copies of the edited manuscript for you to compare with the original. Again, these always arrive at the most inconvenient time and usually have a 48-hour turn around time! It is very important to check the proof copy carefully as some errors can creep into your work in the type-setting stage of publication. Some journals, however, do not send proof copies but Author Queries, and do the editing and proof checking 'in house'. Once you have sent back the proof copy and other forms you wait with anticipation to see the paper in print and most importantly, what reaction it will receive from the scholarly research community.

9

FROM THESIS TO
JOURNAL ARTICLE

- Start early
- What's the market for your research?
- Research methodology and publishing
- One study or a number?
- After the examination
- If you have finished your thesis or research project

Many readers of this book will have either recently completed a doctorate, or will be in the process of completing one, and will be interested in how to turn their thesis into a publication. Indeed, all research theses should see the printer's ink in refereed journal publications, as well as through the more common conference presentations. Other readers will be in the early stages of designing research projects for funding through granting bodies. While the publication process should not drive your research and thesis, I think it is important that you should prepare for publication very early in the process of designing your study and planning the format of your thesis or research reports. In other words, if you don't have a mind to publish your work in the most prestigious journals to disseminate your results, why bother with the research in the first place?

Good doctoral research should provide the next wave of groundbreaking theorising and research in psychology, and so it is very important that this be disseminated as widely as possible. Furthermore, as doctoral degrees are research training degrees, it is only appropriate that a key element of the research process, that of publication of results for peer and community review and usage, be a natural part of the doctoral process.

I am aware that in many, if not most, research degree programs, there is an emphasis on writing an effective thesis, and many books are available to guide the student in this. I have listed a number of these as recommended readings at the end of the chapter. Many of the writing skills learnt in the degree course are, of course, transferable and consistent with the suggestions I have made for research publishing in the earlier chapters in this book. Indeed, the quality of a thesis, as assessed by the examiners, should reflect its publishable quality. However, there are differences between producing a thesis that fulfills the requirements for the award of a degree, completing a research report as part of a grant or consultancy, and writing an effective research article for publication in a respected journal. It is a common experience that graduated students find it difficult to get their research published even though their thesis was highly regarded. It is also a common experience that research reports have difficulty getting published in refereed journals. Among the differences between theses and research reports and journal articles that can cause articles drawn from the former to come to grief during review are length, selectivity, writing style, and interpretation of data (see, *APA Publication Manual*, 4th Edition).

So how to get published? Depending on what stage your thesis or research is at you will have more or less control over the elements I discuss below.

START EARLY

As I indicated above, if you are in the early stages of designing your research you can have an eye to publishing right from the beginning of your study. Early attempts at publishing in peer journals provide you with a number of key advantages. If your articles are accepted for review you will receive invaluable feedback on your work as it is progressing. Modifications and refinements can then be included both in the research design and in the final thesis, even if the submitted article is not accepted for publication. If the articles are accepted for publication it gives significant credibility to your research prior to examination of your thesis. This early attempt at publication will hone your skills at being selective in what you report, being disciplined in the length at which you elaborate, writing in an objective style and with an eye to APA format, and being circumspect in how you interpret your data. Many theses suffer from faults such as excessive wordiness, lack of selectivity in the presentation of results and overinterpretation of results. Hence, refinements learnt through the school of peer review can then be included in your thesis, making it even stronger. Second, if you are writing for an elite readership of prestigious journals your own standards (and those of your mentors and supervisors) for your research will also rise. Third, your final thesis will be in a form that allows further publication without too much reworking and rewriting. I appreciate the fact that some theses and research reports (for example, for consultancies or granting bodies) are constrained by particular requirements and headings, but I believe that you can work within these frameworks to produce material that can be easily translated into a research journal format. I have often cut and pasted from research grant applications and reports material for publication in journal articles.

In order to facilitate publishing progressively as you conduct your research, you should consider a number of elements. First, many psychological theses and other research projects consist of a series of consecutive and interrelated studies. Consider what parts of your research constitute discrete studies and then write your thesis as a series of discrete but interrelated research papers on these studies. I advise my doctoral students to write each study in their thesis as a separate research article (as much as possible, at least). At the same time, however, I also emphasise that the studies need to be seen as interrelated otherwise the thesis may be criticised for lacking integration. I also have them follow the guidelines for research publishing I have discussed throughout this book. Hence, their final thesis is constituted of a number of already written research articles (hopefully some of these have already been published).

There are some provisos on this. You should not multiply studies for publication purposes by arbitrarily dividing a study into sub-parts. Each reported study should be complete and have an integrity of its own. The final thesis may have longer sections dealing with elements such as method, results and so on than appear in a research article, hence you may need to 'edit down' some sections of your thesis. Conversely, you might have major chapters in your thesis dealing with research design from which an abridged relevant version occurs in each chapter and in your research articles.

WHAT'S THE MARKET FOR YOUR RESEARCH?

In order to publish your research you should begin by answering the question: What's the market for my research? In other words you should start identifying key journals early in your research. This will be made easier by completing a comprehensive literature search. You should also reconsider the material covered in Chapter 3 regarding the status of journals and their requirements, as well as publication lag. If you are sending articles out for review in order to inform your thesis you need to submit to journals that have a quick turn around time.

Most of the requirements of journals in your preferred research area should be built into your thesis or research report format at the outset. Here I am referring to details of presentation, as well as to more substantive issues such as your theorising based upon a corpus of literature reflected by the preferred journals and associated publications, the content of your research, your research questions, your hypothesis formulation, your preferred methodological approaches and so on. Do not ultimately be disappointed by going down a research path that has little chance of being attractive to your preferred journals. There are, of course, exceptions. You might be a methodological or theoretical trail-blazer, for example, and develop new theories, techniques and methods. However, in this case you will need to be prepared to make a very strong argument for publishing your work if it doesn't meet the established criteria of particular journals. I am suggesting here a certain level of pragmatism—you can become a trail-blazer more easily when you have a critical mass of published articles behind you. However, if you are bent on leading the way you should still present your manuscript in a form that is likely to be attractive to the preferred journals rather than confront them with how different your work is from the norm. In other words some clear explanatory writing is appropriate and necessary.

RESEARCH METHODOLOGY AND PUBLISHING

I have discussed in Chapter 2, basic and applied, experimental and correlational research among other methodological issues. There is no doubt that some forms of research are more readily published than some other forms. This might be because there are more journals devoted to particular styles of research. For example, in psychology, it is somewhat more difficult to get long, qualitative and small case study studies published than experimental and correlational studies. Key journals in your area of research will have a preference for particular methodologies and substantive issues, and you need to be aware of this. In other words, it is somewhat foolish not to consider the likelihood of where you will publish your work before you begin, and take heed of guidelines applying to those avenues for publication. I can recall vividly the distress of a PhD graduate who, after completing an excellent thesis, failed to have much published from it. The primary reason was that the journals to which she was submitting her study considered her work too small scale to generate much useful, generalisable, information. So, it really is sensible to design a study, or series of studies, which you believe will be appropriate to specific journals. This does not guarantee publication, but at least it is a good start.

ONE STUDY OR A NUMBER?

If you are beginning your research you might also like to consider whether it is strategic to put all your research eggs in one basket, or to have a number of baskets. In other words, you may have some control over whether you design one 'blockbuster' study or a number of studies integrated around a central research question. I will not recommend either approach but I make the point that if you do one study you may get a limited number of publications from it. However, on the converse, the publications that do emanate from a well-conducted and significant study, such as a research monograph, or a very significant research paper, may give you more credibility as a researcher than many less significant articles published by other researchers.

AFTER THE EXAMINATION

In a number of countries a thesis is sent out for external examination and the examiners provide a detailed critique of the research. Students may be required by the examiners to make changes to the research or thesis in order for it to be approved for the award of the degree. In other cases the suggested changes may be optional for inclusion in the thesis. In either case, you should consider the examiners' comments seriously as they form a 'high level' review of your work (often more extensive than you will get through journal reviewers) which should inform any further revision of your work for publication. Rather than being seen as an imposition on you (and you are probably heartily sick of your thesis by then), these changes are likely to help you shape up your research for publication in refereed journals. You ignore them at your peril.

Co-authors

While, in general, your thesis will be attributed to you as sole author, more than likely it has been shaped by a number of people. In the United States and other places it will be your doctoral committee, while in some other places it might be your supervisors. It is also more than likely that you have had other mentors that have helped shape your ideas, refine your method-ologies, and read your progressive chapters. You should harness these people as co-authors on journal article development. In other words, many of these people will already be skilled at the art of getting published and you should seek their advice and help on getting your work published. The issue of the attributing of authorship and order of authorship on articles derived from theses is somewhat thorny, and I will not get into the debate here. You might like to read the *American Psychologist* article by Fine and Kurdek dealing with this issue (November 1993, 48, 1141–7). Most universities have ethics guidelines on this matter which protect the right of the student to be first author on work that is substantially the student's. Having said this, it is also only fair that work done by others in shaping up your thesis for journal publication should be acknowledged either in co-authorship (when the contribution has been substantial and substantive) or in an acknowledgment. My strongest advice here is for you to openly discuss who is to be author and in what order before you get help on the article.

Some readers, not completing research degrees, will be involved in joint research with more senior researchers. The advantage of conducting research with senior researchers is that they should be mentors in helping you write effective research articles. This collaborative research should be very supportive of your personal attempts to get published. However, it is wise to establish early in the research specific responsibilities including those for driving the articles that come from the research. Many collaborative projects fail to have an effective leader who will guide the production of high quality research articles. Hence, little of the research, if any, ends up in articles. Try to develop research projects with people who are not only researchers but actively publishing. Again, it is sensible to negotiate authorship responsibilities for proposed articles and author order on articles that are written.

IF YOU HAVE FINISHED YOUR THESIS OR RESEARCH PROJECT

Even if you have already finished your thesis, or your research project, many of the suggestions above can still be implemented. Let's look at a number of questions you can ask yourself about your thesis in order to ascertain best how to publish from it.

Does your thesis consist of a series of studies or one substantive study? If it is one substantive study it might best be published as a research monograph. In this case it will probably still need to be condensed and rewritten with a tighter theoretical and methodological framework, and a more succinct literature review, presentation and interpretation of results. In other words, very few theses or reports translate effectively into publications for a wider audience without some extensive rewriting. If your thesis or research is comprised of a series of smaller studies there is potential for a number of separate publications. Even if you conducted one holistic study you can write a series of articles based on it for different audiences. For example, you might be able to produce a methodological article and a scholarly research article on the substantive findings, as well as a more 'pop' applied article for practitioners.

What was the original organisation of your thesis? Does your thesis have separate chapters devoted to literature review, method, analyses, findings and discussion or are these elements contained in a brief form within each chapter? If your thesis was written around separate chapters devoted to the methodological elements of the study, develop a template which summarises these that may be used in separate journal articles which report distinct elements of the study and their related findings.

What was the scope and originality of your research project? What new knowledge was generated? Theses, for example, often replicate research. You need to ascertain which aspects of your research are novel and contribute to new knowledge.

Focus your research articles on this 'new knowledge'

Take a careful look at the language and length of your thesis. At times theses are longwinded. You may need to carefully rewrite sections so that they are brief, focused and in the genre of shorter research articles. In particular, you will want to report the most salient aspects of the research (typically theses and research reports present all results). Furthermore, there is a tendency in theses and research reports to over interpret findings. This is natural as authors have invested such a lot of energy and time on their projects. However, over interpreting results is a fatal flaw in research articles and should be avoided at all costs.

There are also some conventions in theses and research reports that are not appropriate in journal articles, such as a 'definitions' section. If you include a definitions section in an article it will be immediately recognised as coming from a thesis. Part of your strategy is to make your article look anything but a re-presentation of a thesis. It is also common in theses and research reports to list endless references so, again, be very selective and choose only the most appropriate for your article.

Good luck with your publishing!

RECOMMENDED READING

American Psychological Association. (1994). *Publication manual of the American Psychological Association*, 4th Edition. Washington, DC: American Psychological Association.
Cone, J. D. & Foster, S. L. (1993). *Dissertations and theses from start to finish. Psychology and related fields*. Washington, DC: American Psychological Association.
Fine, M. A. & Kurdek, L. A. (1993). Reflections on determining authorship credit and authorship order on faculty–student collaboration. *American Psychologist*, 48, 1141–73.
Smyth, T. R. (1996). *Writing in psychology*. 2nd Edition. Brisbane: John Wiley.

CODE OF ETHICS

You might like to consider the following code of ethics for psychological research produced by the Australian Psychological Society. International psychological associations produce similar documents.

SECTION E: RESEARCH

1. In planning psychological research, members must undertake a careful evaluation of the ethical issues involved. Whatever guidance is sought from others, the responsibility for ensuring ethical practice in research remains with the principal investigators and cannot be shared. It is the responsibility of members to ensure that research is conducted in such a manner that the welfare of participants is not compromised.
2. It is a responsibility of members conducting research to comply with guidelines and requirements for ethical accountability in research within their setting such as any current National Health and Medical Research Council Guidelines on Human Experimentation. It is unethical for a member to initiate or undertake research without complying with appropriate ethical procedures.
3. Members must be aware that in all scientific research with human participants, there is a need to balance the welfare of others who ultimately may benefit from the findings of the investigation against any discomfort or risks to participants.

4. Members must preserve and protect the respect and dignity of all participants and endeavour to ensure that participants' consent to be involved in the research is voluntary. Wherever possible, participants must be appropriately informed of the nature and purpose of the investigation. Members must inform participants of the nature of the research and that they are free to participate or to decline to participate or to withdraw from the research. Such informed consent must be appropriately documented.

5. When potential research participants are individuals such as students, employees or subordinates, members must not use a position of authority to exert undue pressure for the purpose of securing their participation in a particular research project. Members must also take special care to protect the prospective participants from adverse consequences of declining or withdrawing from participation.

6. When research participation is a course requirement, the member must ensure that the prospective participant is given the choice of equitable alternative activities.

7. For persons who are legally incapable of giving informed consent, members must provide an appropriate explanation, obtain the participant's consent and obtain appropriate consent from the persons who are legally responsible for participants' welfare.

8. Before deciding that research does not require informed written consent of research participants, members must consult with colleagues or gatekeepers and ethics committees as appropriate.

9. Members must not offer excessive financial or other inappropriate inducements to obtain research participants.

10. When it is necessary for scientific reasons to conduct a study without fully informing participants of its true purpose prior to the commencement of the study, the member must ensure that participants do not suffer distress from the research procedure. Participants must be informed of the purpose of the investigation at the conclusion of the research. Also, members must be careful to maintain the quality of their relationship with participants and to correct any mistaken attitudes or beliefs that participants may have about the research.

11. Wherever possible the procedures for establishing confidentiality must be explained to participants at the outset of the research. Members must obtain informed written consent from research participants if there is to be anticipated further

use of personally identifiable research data. Test results or other confidential data obtained in a research study must not be disclosed in situations or circumstances which might lead to identification of the participants unless their informed written consent has been obtained.

12. The member must take all reasonable steps to ensure that participants are not exposed to risk of injury incidental to the procedures used, for example, from faulty stimulus presentation or recording equipment.

13. When the research necessarily involves participants in physical or mental stress, the member must inform participants concerning the procedures to be used, and the physical and psychological effects to be expected. No research procedures likely to cause severe distress should be used under any circumstances. If unexpected stress reactions of significance occur, the member has the responsibility immediately to alleviate such reactions and to terminate the investigation. If a research procedure involves participants in high levels of emotional arousal, it is incumbent on the member to ensure that no psychologically vulnerable person participates.

14. Members must anticipate the subsequent effects of research participation and provide information on services available for participants to alleviate any unnecessary distress that follows from their participation. Members must not engage in other professional relationships with research participants in relation to resolving any such distress.

15. When working in a multidisciplinary research team or other context in which members do not have sole decision-making authority, they must make these ethical principles known to other members of the research team or other decision-makers, and seek their adoption prior to engaging in the research.

16. Members must provide an opportunity for participants to obtain appropriate information about the nature, results, and conclusion of the research.

17. Members must make provisions for maintaining confidentiality in the access, storage and disposal of research data, subject to the legal requirements of their institutions.

18. Members must take all reasonable steps to minimise the discomfort, illness and pain of animals. The care of laboratory animals must be directly supervised by a person competent to ensure their comfort, health and humane treatment, and the care and use of animals in research must be consistent with National Health and Medical Research Council Statement on Animal Experimentation.

SECTION F: REPORTING AND PUBLICATION OF RESEARCH
RESULTS

1. Members must not fabricate data or falsify results in their publications. If members discover significant errors in their publications they must take reasonable steps to correct such errors in an appropriate manner.
2. Members must not present substantial portions or elements of another's work or data as their own.
3. Authorship is assigned to persons only for work they have actually performed or to which they have contributed.
4. Minor contributions may be acknowledged in a footnote or in an introductory statement. In each case the author(s) must obtain a contributor's consent before including his or her name. Multiple authors are responsible for specifying the order in which their names appear on the title page. Where a member is given access to data collected and owned by another researcher or group of researchers, authorship must be mutually agreed before the commencement of data analysis.
5. A student is usually listed as principal author on any multiple-authored article that is substantially based on the student's dissertation or thesis. The student's supervisor will usually be second author to such a publication. If the student does not submit a manuscript for publication in a reasonable period of time after completion of the research ['reasonable period' should be determined by the Psychology Academic Organisational Unit (AOU) Head], then the supervisor may publish the research and assume primary authorship and the student must be listed as an author.
6. Members must not publish, as original data, data that have been previously published. Data can be republished when they are accompanied by proper acknowledgment. Data must be kept after publication in accordance with the member's institutional requirements.
7. After research results are published or publicly available, members must not withhold the data on which their conclusions are based from other competent professionals who seek to verify the substantive claims through reanalysis and who intend to use such data only for that purpose, provided that the confidentiality of the participants can be protected.
8. Members who review material submitted for publication, grant, or other research proposal review must respect the

confidentiality of and the proprietary rights in such information of those who submitted it.

9. Members must declare any vested interest in their research including acknowledgment of funding sources and other interests in the research.

INDEX

abstract, the 14–16
  APA style for 37
  of basic and applied research
    14–16
  of correlational research 20
  of experimental research 17–18
  of integrative review 25
  of meta-analysis 26
  of qualitative research 23–4
  of quasi-experimental research
    19
  style of 43, 44–6
  of validation studies 21–2
acceptance, letter of 115–16, 128
acknowledgments 48, *see also*
  references
American Psychological
  Association Publication
  Manual, *see* APA style
  essentials/guidelines
American Psychological Society
  7, 9
APA (American Psychological
  Association)
  Ethical Principles 43
  style essentials/guidelines
    35–42, 111
  web site 67–9
appendixes 48–50
applied research 12, 13
article, research 35–51, Chapters
  4, 5, 6 and 9. *See also*
  discussion; literature review;
  method section; results;

submitting research for
  publication
  response to Chapter 8, *see also*
    letters/replies; reviewers
  revising 116–28

basic and applied research 12–16
Basic and Applied Social Psychology
  13, 14, 31–2, 34

citations, text 38–40
code of ethics 9, 137–41
confidentiality 138, 139, 140–1
correlational research 19–21,
  132, 133
credit, publication 9–10
Culture and Psychology 53

data, sharing 10
data bases 65–7
definitions/descriptors 69–70, 136
design, research 6, 26, 75–6
discussion presented in research
  article 47–8, 95–7
dual/multiple authorship 10–11,
  134–5
duplicate publication 8–9, 10,
  111

*Educational and Psychological
  Measurement* 32
errors, correction of proofreading
  9, 98, 128
ethical standards/guidelines 7–10,
  43, 134, 137–41

and authorship 140
and confidentiality 138, 139,
    140–1
and human participants 137–9
reporting and publication of
    results 140–1
and use of animals 139
experimental research 16–18, 84,
    132–3

format, *see* style and format

guidelines/instructions
    for authors 92–3, *see also*
        ethical standards; style and
        format
    for reviewers 104–10

hypotheses 71, 72–3

instruments, research 80–4
    and literature review 63–5
    and observational studies 82–4
    special equipment 84
    surveys and questionnaires
        80–1
integrative reviews 24–5
Internet, *see* World Wide Web

joint research 134–5
journals
    access on World Wide Web 32
    circulation of 33
    citations of 33–4
    mission statements of 29–31
    prestige/status of 32–4, 132
    requirements/preferences of
        42–3, 51–5
    review process 33, Chapters 7
        and 8, *see also* reviewers
    reviewers, *see* reviewers
    selection of 28–34, 132
    types of 28–32
    Web sites 32, 69
Journal of Educational Psychology
    34, 58
*Journal of Personality and Social
    Psychology* 29–31, 51

length of manuscript 52–3

letters/replies from journals
    acceptance 115–16, 128
    rejection 112, 113–15
    'revise and resubmit' 115–20,
        see also revising research
        article
literature review 5–6, Chapter 4
    and descriptors 69–70
    and hypotheses 71, 72, 72–3
    and instruments/techniques
        63–5
    and previous/related research
        59, 61
    purpose of 57–65, 71
    and research questions 59, 71
    and research sources 65–9
    and theoretical models 62–3
    and types of publications
        searched 70

market/potential for publication
    26, 132
meta-analyses 24–6, 77
method section of article 46–7,
    Chapter 5
    analyses 85–8
    instruments 80–4
    participants/subjects 76–80
    procedures 85
    research design 6, 26, 75–6
methodologies, research Chapter
    2, 132–3
    appropriateness of 3–5

pagination 36, 37, 40
participants in research, *see*
    subjects/participants
plagiarism 8, 9
presentation, styles of 35–51, *see
    also* style and format
procedures and analyses 85–8
proofreading article 98, 128
publication
    duplicate 8–9
    potential for 26, 132, *see also*
        journals
    presenting research for 51–6,
        see also article; journals,
        selection of; style and
        format; submitting research

publication credit 9–10

qualitative research 22–4
quasi-experimental research 16–18
questionnaires 80–1
questions, research 59, 71, 90–1
quotations 40, *see also* references

references 40–2, 50–1, 97–8
rejection, letter of 112, 113–15
research
    basic and applied 12–16, 132
    design 6, 26, 75–6
    and ethical standards, *see*
        ethical standards/guidelines
    major types of Chapter 2
    market for 26,132, *see also*
        journals
    methodologies, *see* research
        methods/methodologies
    purpose of 57–65, 71
    questions and hypotheses 59,
        71, 72, 90–1
    results, *see* results, publishing
    scientific 1–2
    sources 65–70
    stages 5–6, *see also* research
        methods; Chapter 9
    value of 1–5
research methods/methodologies
    3–5, 16–21, 132–3, *see also*
    method section of article
    basic and applied 12–16
    correlational research 19–21,
        132, 133
    experimental research 16–18,
        132–3
    quasi-experimental research
        18–19
results, publishing 47, Chapter 6
    and code of ethics 140–1
    reporting 9, 90–1
    and research questions 90–1
    statistical presentation 92–3
    and tables and figures 91–2
review, peer 99–100, 110
review process 33, Chapters 7
    and 8

reviewers, journal 10, 100–10,
    Chapter 8
    guidelines/instructions for
        104–10
    comments on research articles
        117, 119–27, *see also*
        letters/replies
    responding to comments of
        116–28
revising research article 116–28

scientific research 1–2
search engines, WWW 67–9
sources, research 65–70
statistical presentation 92–3
style and format 35–51
    guides 35–43
    special requirements of
        journals 42–3
    typical format 43–51
subjects/participants in research
    76–80
    demographic information
        79–80
    and ethical standards 137–9
    non-human 80, 139
    selecting 77–9
submitting research for
    publication 51–6, *see also*
    article; style and format;
    journal, selection of
surveys and questionnaires 80–2

tables and figures 91–2
thesis, the Chapter 9
    and co-authors 134–5
    examiner's critique 133–4
    and originality of research 135
    and starting the article 130–2
title page 36–7, 44

validation studies 21–2
value of research 1–5

World Wide Web
    APA style guide on 35–6
    data bases 65–7
    journals on 32, 69
    search engines/sites 67–9